T0043850

Strange to Say

Strange to Say

Etymology as Serious Entertainment

DEBORAH WARREN

PAUL DRY BOOKS
Philadelphia 2021

First Paul Dry Books Edition, 2021

Paul Dry Books, Inc.
Philadelphia, Pennsylvania
www.pauldrybooks.com

Copyright © 2021 Deborah Warren

All rights reserved.

ISBN 978-1-58988-157-0

Printed in the United States of America

Library of Congress Control Number: 2021942497

I dedicate this book to Rhina Espaillat
with love, gratitude, and her own words:
Mundo Y Palabra / The World and the Word

Contents

An Invitation

You don't have to read this book straight through. Open it anywhere and dip into a couple of pages. Virgil fans used this technique with the *Aeneid*, landing haphazardly on a verse they could interpret as prophecy or advice. People did the same with the Bible a few centuries later. (The millennia have come up with some strange methods for getting intel on the future; I personally would choose *margaritomancy*—divination by bouncing pearls.) Not that this book is one hundred percent comparable in stature to the *Aeneid* or the Bible.

Etymology = evolution: language is all about mutation. Like evolution, this book has no agenda—because who knows where any word is headed? And, like evolution, I occasionally meander etymologically (the *Meander* being a looping Turkish river). As with evolution of living organisms (which they are), words, without design or purpose or end-goal, ooze along like blind amoebae.

You might not care about Syphilis the shepherd boy, or the number of calories burnt by laughter, or the Worshipful Company of Security Professionals, or where we get biscuits, bagels, éclairs, and other hand-helds, or the demented mondegreens and malapropisms that don't get into our permanent lexical DNA. But, speaking of pearls, words are jewels—"little things that delight": the word *jewel* derives from Latin *iocus* ("joke or play"). Later on, *jocus* produced Italian *gioia* ("joy") and *gioiello* ("jewel"). Indeed, à propos of valuables, a language is a *treasury* (from Greek *thesaurus*).

And à propos of treasure, etymology is a gold-mine of slip-ups that do settle into our verbal genes. Take Cinderella's glass slippers. In the original tale, they were made of *vair* ("fur")—which in the orally-told story mistakenly turned into the homonym *verre* ("glass"), which is what stuck, as a nice bonus feature of the fairy tale.

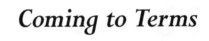

Coming to Terms

1

In a Word

Evolution

Besides the double helix in your chromosomes—your personal mess of nucleotides, saccharides and phosphates—you inherited an insubstantial third strand from a parallel genome: language.

As with genes, however, no sooner do we inherit a word than it changes:

▶ *For Lack of a Better Word:* Maybe it designates something new in terms of something that already exists—like *horsepower*, the work done by one horse (which, as you know, is 550 foot-pounds/sec). Or *dumbwaiter*, which one company had to rename "service lift" after complaints that *dumbwaiter* was derogatory. Or the gym *dumbbell*, a handbell-shaped thing that doesn't ring. Or printing something from your laptop: *print* literally meant "to *im*print or press," and there's none of that going on with your LaserJet.

▶ *Say No More:* Maybe a word (*candlepower*, say) coexists with a new rival only temporarily, pretty much petering out when it's no longer the top option, like Neanderthal man, who lived for a while alongside modern humans. The International System of Units defines one candlepower, though obsolete, as 0.981 candelas. If some sort of nostalgia prompts you to use it, a candela is "luminous intensity, in a given direction, of a source that emits monochromatic radiation of frequency 540 × 1012 Hz and that has a radiant intensity in that direction of 1/683 watt per steradian."

▶ **Spreading the Word:** Or maybe a word gradually diverges across isolated groups, the way Darwin's species of finches evolved differently on separate islands. Thus when the Roman Empire fizzled out, it left behind, in its various provinces, Latin that split into diverse Romance languages, isolated by circumstances like mountains and lack of dissemination by communications media.

Changing words evolved into *cognates* of each other—etymological cousins with a common ancestry. In each region they gradually coalesced into a *vernacular*: "native language" (from *verna*, "domestic-born slave").

Example: While English is constipated with consonants (a legacy of Anglo-Saxon), the lazy French tongue transformed Latin into more fluid sounds. Any time the French didn't have enough to do, they passed the time by throwing another silent *e* into a word. Just kidding; their "mute *e*" came from Latin's inflected endings. But it's largely that characteristic that makes their syllables flow smoothly where ours are often relatively thick and lumpy.

▶ **Slip of the Tongue:** Or maybe a mutation starts with an error of the ear. The deranged mondegreens and malapropisms mentioned above are one-offs that never go genetic.

You're already thinking of ways where the gene conceit breaks down, but we won't leave it before three sentences on *DNA*. Your personal recipe has one ingredient: *deoxyribose nucleic acid*. We get *ribose* from *arabinose*—*gum arabic*, an Arabian plant-sap. We get *nucleus* from *nux*, "nut or kernel." We get *acid* from *oxys*, "sharp or bitter."

And now we draw a veil over any actual hard science.

2

Double-Speak
Anglo-Latin

First, a word about the word "English." *England* and *angler* (as in fishing) share a common source: "fish-hook." The *Angle* people were natives of *Angeln*, the hook-shaped Danish peninsula; they kept invading fifth-century England until it became *Angle-land.* (The story goes that around 600 A.D., Pope Gregory I, seeing some golden-haired Angle slaves, allegedly punned: "not Angles but angels"—*angelus*, "messenger/angel.") The Angles and Saxons gave us forty percent of our words. Latin indirectly gave us most of the rest.

We'll get specific in the third chapter, but first a synopsis of Britain's linguistic heritage—probably already familiar to you:

Before the Roman Empire unraveled, Saint "The Rock" Peter had christened the Eternal City as the go-to place; all roads led to Rome. But by the early fifth century, the Romans had quit Britain. Even during Roman occupation, rustics in their wattle-and-daub huts had tilled and toiled on, largely ignorant of Roman garrisons. Never exposed to Latin, they went on speaking what they'd inherited from Celts and early Norse settlers. Then, unlike the Roman soldiery, the Angles and various Saxon tribes who overran England mingled with the locals, who increasingly spoke *Anglo-Saxon*, also known as *Old English.*

As an aside on Peter as "rock": during the Gold Rush, a vein of ore *petered out* as it was mined.

English didn't acquire its Latin-based words until five centuries later—in the form of French. In 1066 Britain was conquered by the Normans ("Norsemen"), originally Vikings who had populated northwestern France. The Normans, who became the British nobility, were francophones, much like the eighteenth-century Russian aristocracy.

Between 1066 and 1500, the *Old English* of the countryside evolved into *Middle English*. Over this half-millennium (don't forget the second *n* in *millennium*, from Latin *annus*, "year"; one *n* and you have Latin *anus*, "ring." Spelled the same but pronounced differently, *anus* also means "old woman," whose English adjective is "anile" as opposed to "anal").

Anyway, the athletic English language often developed two different terms for the same thing. Where the rural classes used an Anglo-Saxon word, the Norman rulers and the educated upper class used a Latinate one. Hence we have *fieldwork/ agriculture, sweat/perspire, plough/cultivator, byre/stable, dirt/soil, dig/excavate, rug/carpet, dish/plate.*

Middle English would be hard for us to understand. *Fate* was pronounced "fat." *Boot* sounded like "boat." Both *ride* and *red* were "reed." If your name is Reid, you may have a ginger-haired medieval ancestor called Reid, who was probably a distant descendant of the red-headed Neanderthals of Germany's Neander valley—I won't travel back as far as the auburn *orangutan*, "forest man." Or do you have *Titian* hair? In northern Italy, including Venice where Titian worked, there were plenty of strawberry blonds.

The *boat*-to-*boot* change was part of the Great Vowel Shift (GVS to us insiders) between the fourteenth and seventeenth centuries. The details are not our business here, unless you're into monophthongization and tables with funny symbols like *aʊ* and /ɛː/.

What about consonants? As only one example, English often swaps German *b* to *v*: *Sieben*/seven; *Leben*/live; *Halb*/half;

Lieben/love. Similarly, Hebrew *Elizabeth* became not only Italian *Elisabetta* but also Russian *Elizavetta*.

Owing to our human oral equipment, *b* and *v* also switch around in the Romance languages. When closing the lips to say *BR* was just too much work, Gallic mouths changed *b* to *v* (or *f*). The French like their *r* at the back of the palate, verging on a *k* sound. Thus February became French *février* and *gubernatorial* affairs concern "governors." *PR*, too: our April is French *avril*. The Italians (so what if Latin was their home turf?) were allergic to *PT*, so *Neptune* becomes *Nettuno* and *baptist battista*, whereas French splits the difference by just not pronouncing the written *p*: baptism = *ba[p]tême*. As for the Spanish, they make no distinction at all; *v* sounds the same as *b*. As Latin quips, *Beati hispani, quibus vivere bibere est* (lucky Spaniards, for whom to live is to drink).

So without leaving the sofa, you can board a time machine and hear history-in-the-making: just let your lips travel backward from consonant to consonant.

Warning to non-philologists: On that time machine, pause at 500 B.C.E., shift into reverse, and get out fast. When I tell you that h_2melg is the Proto-Indo-European root for *milk*, you see why this book stops well short of PIE (as *cognoscenti* style it)—a conjectured extinct language spoken six thousand years ago, the ancestor of all Indo-European languages. Take, for example, Germanic *way* and Latin *via*; we trace both back to their common PIE forefather *wegh*. But to you and me, PIE will remain *terra incognita*. Not being an academic, I wonder whether, at their professional powwows, PIE scholars actually *say* "pie."

If the Roman legions in Britain left little Latin behind, they did leave physical legacies such as defense walls like *Hadrian's* ("Adriatic guy"). And you can still see the mosaics (origin Greek *muse*) of villa floors. London was *Londinium*, where, speaking of pie, one major Roman road became today's Pye Road. London's modern transportation complex, and I use the term advisedly, is the Underground, or *Tube* (which in America is the TV, namely the *cathode ray tube*). To Londoners, of course, it's the *chyoob*.

Speaking of TV, in 1958 Pius XII retroactively, and who minds a little anachronism, declared St. Clare of Assisi (b. 1194) the patron saint of television. Taking a sick day at home, Clare viewed Mass in a private vision on her bedroom wall.

Tubes. For the Romans, the *tuba* was a war-trumpet. More interesting: Latin *tromba*, "trumpet," became the *trombone*, and the French took its name for their similarly shaped "paperclip."

The Tube has already taken us more than a few stations from Anglo-Latin vocabulary, but pardon another parenthesis while we're discussing instruments: The *piano* started out as the *pianoforte* which, unlike the harpsichord, lets you modulate dynamics from soft (*piano*) to loud (*forte*). Italian, the language of music, also gave us the *piccolo*, "little flute" (see *-olus* below).

Then there's the stuff an instrument's made of. *Xylem* ("wood") produced the *xylophone*. We got *viola* from *vitula*—the calf who gave its guts for strings. (As for violins, in French a "hobby" is a *violon d'Ingres*: to relax from his day job as a painter, Ingres played the violin. Our English *hobby* started as "hobbyhorse.") The *violin* was a small *viola*, a *violino*. And size is our next topic.

Talking Big. Many English words reflect the efficient Latinate suffixes for denoting size. Italian *-one* usually means "big"; *-one* derives from Latin *-umn*, where a *columna* ("column") is a "big neck" (neck = *collum*, as in "collar"). *Auctumnus* ("autumn") = "the big harvest," a term related to "auction"; in fact, *increase* was once a term for "crops." The *-one* ending gives us tromb*one*, "large trumpet." *Al Capone*'s surname suggests an ancestor with a large *capo* ("head") and is also a good fit for a *caporegime*—the head of a gang. The *capo di tutti capi*, "head of all the heads," is the Mafia CEO, where "chief executive officer" is also a particularly apt title. A Mafia boss is also called a *padrone*—"big father."

Another term for a big shot is a *mogul*, the seventeenth-century European name for the great Mongol, a former Asian emperor.

Small Talk. Going small, Latin appends *-ulus* or *-olus*. Here, for instance, is Paracelsus in 1537 on how to make a *homunculus*, a miniature but fully-formed man. He specifies

> that the sperm of a man be putrefied by itself in a sealed cucurbit for forty days with the highest degree of putrefaction in a horse's womb, or at least so long that it comes to life and moves itself, and stirs . . . it will look somewhat like a man, but transparent . . . If, after this, it be fed wisely with the Arcanum of human blood, and be nourished for up to forty weeks, and be kept in the even heat of the horse's womb, a living human child grows therefrom . . . like another child, which is born of a woman, but much smaller.

"Muscle" derives from *mus* ("mouse"): a *musculus* is a "little mouse" that appears to move under your skin. Count *Dracula* is a little *draco*, Latin for "dragon." A molecule is a "small mass." Your *uncle* began his career as *avunculus*—a not-quite *avus*, "forebear." A *regulation* is a "little rule."

This *-ul* is to blame for making *nucular* sound so right. But, while it's true that a *nucula* is a "little nut," the kernel of that nut is its *nucleus*. A nucleus is the kernel or core of an atom: we can't nuke *nuclear*. Knowing Latin vocabulary always helps in cases like these. Example: many speakers butcher *integral*. So what if—like *integrity*—it's based on *integer*, "one, whole"? It becomes *intregal* or *intergal*. A third option appears on the wall of the "Intergrative Medicine" clinic I once visited. Painted in foot-high letters.

Our English "small" is German *schmal*, "slender." Another form of *-ulus* is *-ellum*. Thus a *cerebellum* is a smaller *cerebrum*.

Porcellus = "piglet." A Germanic *Margret* is nicknamed *Gretel*. There's also *Hansel* of the clever sylvan GPS; too bad the birds pinched the bits of bread.

3

From the Word Go

Word Gets Around

Around the fourteenth century, the modern meaning of "travel" grew out of the French *travail* (labor or toil), from *tripalium*, an instrument of torture, in turn from *palus*, "stake"; hence our "palisade" and "beyond the pale."

Travel as torture? Surely this is *hyperbole*—i.e., "throwing beyond," from Greek *ballein*, "to throw." The common root of *ballein* and *ball* goes way back to "swelling" (the PIE territory where dilettantes do not venture). Their cousin *phallus*, for example, is a swollen item.

Automotive Etymologies. A *coupe*, which we call a "coop," was once a *carrosse coupé*, a "cut carriage," where one of the seats was removed.

"Cab" stems from French *cabriolet*, which was not our yellow object but a light well-sprung carriage. *Cabriolet* (from *capra*, Latin "goat") derives from a goat's springy leap, as in "caper." Recall, *en passant*, the horned celestial goat *Capricorn*—plus two movie surnames, Leonardo DiCaprio and director Frank Capra. By the way, goats *browse* (on brush); it's sheep and cows that *graze* (on grass). And we get the brand *Chevrolet* from the French *chèvre* (goat), or maybe, via a *b/v* swap, from *cabriolet*, right? Wrong! Chevy's producer just happened to be a man named Louis Chevrolet, who probably never thought of himself as an etymological little goat.

In the seventeenth century, the Hôtel de Saint Fiacre in Paris rented carriages; soon *fiacre* evolved into any French cab. More importantly, this same Fiacre is the patron saint of hemorrhoids (known as "St. Fiacre's figs") and of stress, cancer, and calamities.

Taxis (*taxi-*, Greek for "transport") bring to mind the Uber-Cab, now Uber—from German *über,* cognate to "upper, over, and above." An UberCab = a superior cab.

Last but not least lengthwise, there's the *limo.* The *limousine* began as clothing—a cloak, named for its region of origin, *Limousin,* which then gave its name to the once-roofless car when a new covered model replaced the traditional open one. The *Limousin* was known for its capital *Limoges,* the biggest French porcelain producer.

The Word on the Street. Talking of travel, let's turn to intersections. A French *patte d'oie* ("goose foot") refers not only to "crow's feet" around the eyes but also to an intersection of roads or paths. Here let's return briefly back to travel as torture.

Intersections were dangerous places in the olden days. With no signage (a word—and there are plenty more—not used by the best people) it was easy to take the wrong fork. A trip today has more hassles than hazards; but old-time travel was hell. You might as well just go straight *to* Hell, which sometimes you literally did—because you could easily succumb to a journey's natural or felonious dangers.

Intersections were convenient spots for ambushes. Enter Diana of the Crossroads, an alter ego of the Roman goddess *Trivia,* "three roads." Diana covered three locales: The patroness of wild things on earth, she was also, in heaven, the moon, and in Hades the witch *Hecate* ("she who operates from afar"). At intersections the canny traveler built shrines to Diana. She had a taste for dogs, so you sacrificed puppies to her. She also liked a nice piece of mullet—a fish, not the hairstyle (and I'd wear a fish on my head sooner than a *mullet* haircut).

That was in the forest. In a Roman city, however, an intersection where three paths crossed was a *trivium*—a public meeting place, which produced the word *trivial*, "commonplace."

Besides Hecate loitering with intent at lonely crossroads, elsewhere you had to contend with highwaymen. In the Middle Ages, trees were often cleared to a bowshot's distance from the road to foil *ambushes* by brigands hiding in the bushes. A *footpad* was a pedestrian robber on your *pad*, which means "path" in Dutch. *Bandit* does not refer to a band of thieves, or to their face-covering. *Banditti* were outlaws who had been "banished." A *desperado* is desperate—hopeless (from *sperare*, "hope"). When he attacks you, his *raid* is close kin to *road* and *ride* (from *reita*).

If you had to exchange your tired horses for fresh ones, you learned that inns were a magnet for unsavory personnel. And who says there even *was* an inn within miles of wherever you found yourself benighted? You tried to plan your trip in stages between hostelries, but if things went pear-shaped en route, you'd be lucky to find a 3 × 3-foot shepherd's hut.

In ancient times you often had to rely on the hospitality of locals—so vital for wayfarer welfare that it was a sacred mandate.

Latin *hospes* means both "host" and "guest"—go figure, but actually don't bother: The double meaning reflects the reciprocity of the two roles. It's derived from *hostis*, "enemy" or "stranger." A *hospital* (from *hospes*) was originally a homeless shelter, not associated with illness.

For the Greeks, the *fiat* (Latin, "let it be so") of hospitality toward voyagers had a name: *xenia* (*xenos* = "stranger")—or *theoxenia* when the guests were gods, and hopefully you were lucky enough to recognize them as such. The book of Hebrews says, "Be not forgetful to entertain strangers: for thereby some have entertained angels unawares." Letting louche unknowns into your house sounds like pushing altruism pretty far, but

like the Golden Rule, it was a mutual deal. Someday the travel-
worn shoe will be on the other foot.

To digress *exempli gratia* ("as an example," or *e.g.*): when
Zeus and Hermes disguised themselves as travelers to test one
town's hospitality, everyone turned them away except Baucis
and Philemon. The two gods turned the couple's hovel into a
temple, not neglecting to sweep the rest of the impious village
away in a flood. As a bonus, the pair got to live on after death in
the form of an entwined oak and linden.

Hermes, by the way, gave his name indirectly to *hermetic*;
alchemists credited him with inventing an airtight seal. Her-
meticism was a secret philosophy, closed to the uninitiated,
which included such disciplines as astrology and magic. The
connection with Hermes? The tenets of this philosophy were
those of Hermes Trismegistus, who was a mythical mash-up
of our Hermes and the Egyptian god Thoth—a baboon-headed
individual blessed with a captivating name.

But we were talking about the mutual obligation of hospitality. When communities were scattered and isolated, and the
wayfarer and host didn't personally know each other, xenophobia was almost a default attitude: no media and jet travel to fos-
ter an ounce of globalization.

Breaches of hospitality were common. Sometimes spectac-
ular breaches. I can't recall her psycho-political motive, but in
the Book of Judges, Jael, the wife of Heber the Kenite, gave her
guest—Sisera the Canaanite—"butter in a lordly dish," an exem-
plary hostess until she "took a nail of the tent, and took an
hammer in her hand, and went softly unto him, and smote the
nail into his temples, and fastened it into the ground: for he was
fast asleep and weary. So he died." As a more recent example of
the import of hospitality, take Macbeth. In his case, he knew his
victim perfectly well, so xenophobia doesn't apply. Macbeth initially balks at murder not merely because Duncan is his relative
and his king: the big problem is that he's Duncan's "host/Who
should against his murderer shut the door/Not bear the knife

myself." A third, yet more recent, violation: In 2015, despite the *Pashtunwali* ethical code mandating hospitality even to enemies, Taliban guests murdered their host.

You could often come up with some lame casuistry as a way around the hospitality injunction. To kill your guest Bellerophon is taboo (from *tabu* in Proto-Oceanic) for which hell's Furies would punish you. So you send him on a deadly quest. You're merely using the King David maneuver: get rid of Bathsheba's inconvenient husband (Uriah the Hittite) by telling Joab: "Set ye Uriah in the forefront of the hottest battle, and retire ye from him, that he may be smitten, and die."

Talking of hospitality, *hostel* (short for "hospital") and *hotel* are first cousins. Old French, relatively fresh from Latin, still managed to get its tongue around the Romans' *st*. But modern French flinched; the Lazy Tongue dropped the *s*. The French often memorialize it with a circumflex over the vowel preceding the phantom *s*: Hostel became *hôtel*; castellum, *château*; festum, *fête*; gustus ("taste"), *goût*. *Magister* became *maître*; your *maître d'* (the *maître d'hôtel*, hotel-master) sports two circumflexes.

The *st* survived in *restaurant*, which "restores" your body. British pronunciation of *restaurant*, incidentally, acknowledges the French by ditching the final *t* and saying "rest-straw."

The French found an initial *st-* particularly galling and gradually replaced it with *ét-*. What's *straight* to us is *étroit* to them (it was French colonists who named *Détroit*—a town on a *strait*, which is a narrow thing, as is a *straitjacket*). Latin *stella* slid into Old French *estoile* and then modern *étoile*. Old French *estage* > *étage*. *Escran* > *écran*. It was, on the other hand, the earlier versions that the Normans brought to England in 1066, and the muscular English tongue was fine with *stellar*, *stage*, and *screen*.

In Italian, *st* at the beginning of a word is one case of what they call *impure s*. This is rather hard on the innocent *s*, when it was their own Latin language that gave them *st* in the first place. Still, the reason Italian is so mellifluous (flowing like honey) is its avoidance of consonant clumps. It even has a special definite article (*lo*) to replace *il* before a word beginning with *s* plus a consonant: *lo sport, lo psicologo.* English needs poets to gussy it up into something *glissando.*

If Words Could Kill. In a *campaign* (from Latin *campus* "field," "ground"), you travel to a field of battle. Political candidates also go out into the field and speak on the *hustings* (Norse *hus-ting* = "house assembly"; a *ting*—"unit" or "entity"—is cousin to English "thing").

In the Middle Ages, your nobility was defined by the right to fight—the peasantry could not own arms—and to do so on horseback. In Germany, a knight was called a *ritter* ("rider"). Only a tiny stratum of the medieval population could afford to own horses (*if wishes were horses, beggars would ride*). A *squire* (abbreviation of *esquire*) descends from Latin *equus*, "horse." A squire could afford country property, and therefore horses. An up-and-coming squire might become an *eques* (Latin)—a horseman who was a knight.

Horsemanship brought *chivalry*, from French *cheval*, "horse," which descends from the Latin *cabellus*, another word for "horse" (note *cabellus* > *cheval*'s two French evolutions: *c* > *ch* and *b* > *v*). *Cavalry* is a cognate of "chivalry." A well-born man joined the cavalry; youths or lower-class men were *infantry.* Today, "infantry" are still foot-soldiers, and "cavalry" still ride (tanks, etc.).

Motor Mouth. Nowadays even civilians can procure military transport. Consider General Motors' *Humvee* (High Mobility Multipurpose Wheeled Vehicle), "a four-wheel-drive military automobile" also suitable for any private citizen with plenty of swagger and extensive parking facilities. Or the *Harrier*, which stems from *hergian*—an Anglo-Saxon term for Viking ravages—and which "flies head on fearlessly into the future, exploring new boundaries," which is exactly what I require in a car. The

Harrier eventually mutated into the *Lexus*. Or, as a Toyota site elaborates, "*Harrier* is a only named called in Japan, it is called Lexus RX in the world."

Jeep is a contraction of G.P.—General Purpose vehicle, like *Veep* for V.P.—Vice President.

Volkswagen names are less militant. The "people's car" is all about winds and currents. VW models include: *Scirocco* (Mediterranean desert wind), *Passat* (German trade wind), and *Polo* (polar wind), plus *Jetta* and *Golf* (Jet and Gulf Streams).

And then there are cars that go for a cosmopolitan vibe in a senselessly misspelt Italian city—the *Sienna* or the *Sorento*.

Before cars, only the rich traveled in coaches (horse-drawn). Merchants sought out the "carriage trade," i.e., upper-class big spenders.

No access to hooves or even wagon-wheels? Then you were stuck close to home—at least until the advent of public transport like the bus, first written *'bus*, from Latin *omnibus*: "for all." At the end of the nineteenth century some of the English rural population had exchanged agricultural for industrial servitude and were ready to embrace the first omnibus when it appeared.

4

Putting Words in My Mouth
Eat Your Words

Bread, cousin to German *brot*, is the "staff of life" (parenthetically, the old plural of *staff* was *staves*). The Germanic source of "bread" is *brewth*: like beer, it involves fermentation.

In the Christian Lord's Prayer "daily bread" shows bread's meaning as sustenance. It's so essential that *bread* and *dough* are terms for money—earned by the *breadwinner*. The word *lord* evolved from the elegant Old English *hláfweard*, "loaf warden." *Lady* stems from *hlaefdige*, "loaf kneader," where -*dige* relates to "dough"; -*dige* also evolved into "dairy," another domain of the home-maker. The origin of *woman* is *wimman*, a corruption of "wife-man."

Bagel, too, has a Germanic source, *beygl* being Yiddish for "ring." (À propos of jewelry and Germany, Göring kept a bowl of diamonds on his desk to play with as worry beads.)

Denmark gave us the *Danish*, a pastry which they should have kept. The world is richer, on the other hand, for the French *croissant* = a "crescent," Latin for "increasing," like a crescent moon or a crescendo. Amidst much controversy, today's Brits are straightening the croissant to make it easier to marmalade up. The crescent shape requires three whole knife-strokes, and they have better ways to spend their time. (*Marmalade's* close relative is Greek "honey" + "apple": *meli* + *malum*. And you'll read below why Eve's alleged "apple" was as false as Cinderella's glass slipper.)

Not to overlook Italy and dough, *pizza*, unastonishingly, means "pie" and is probably cognate to the flat *pita* bread. The hamburger *patty* began not as meat but as bread. *Patty* refers to the bun: a small cake of dough, or "paste" (from Latin *pasta*).

On pie: *To eat humble pie* did not start the way we thought. Peasants once ate pie made of *umbles*—the guts of game animals, fare not found on the elegant table. *Umbles* were *offal*—what "falls off" when you trim the meat. *Umble* made for a nice pun, since the *h* in "humble" was once silent. Eventually everyone except Cockneys voiced the *h*, but "umbles" had decayed out of the language. We get today's *humble* from Latin *humilis*, an adjective for *humus*, soil.

Doughnut, now. Why *nut*? Because the first doughnut was a small nutlike orb of fried dough, much like the modern *doughnut hole* you get after flattening the small dough-ball into a disk and *ho*llowing out its center. (*Center* derives from Greek *kentron*—a wasp's stinger or a sharp point.)

Anyway, a "hole" is a nothing, even if it's as vast as an astronomical black hole, which measures "25 magnitudes of extinction." Unfortunately, the Dutch term for doughnut is less gas and more oil: *olykoek* ("oil-cake")—while accurate—lacks appeal.

For charm, give me the *Pillsbury Doughboy*, who embodies our affection for dough. Surveying anthropomorphic food icons, however, I'm even fonder of the *Stay Puft Marshmallow Man*, despite the ominous obesity of his billowing belly. As for the *Michelin Man*, an anti-obesity regimen must account for his updated 2008 body—he's still a pile of tires, but thinned down from the roly-poly 1894 version. Nowadays the spare tires are around your waist. The Michelin Man has a name: *Bibendum*, from Latin *nunc est bibendum*—"it's time for a drink." No one fretted about a little drunk-driving back in nineteenth-century France, where OUI means "Yes!" But what Michelin's Bibendum signified was: This tire drinks up (absorbs) road obstacles, which mattered when dirt roads were a puncture-paradise. Of course (speaking of obesity and tires), Michelin also rates restaurants.

No one got fat on *manna*. This "bread from heaven," sent down to the Israelites in the wilderness, has become a synonym for an unexpected godsend. Various scholars claim the actual manna was tamarisk-tree resin, or honey from insect bodies, or weird flaky stuff resembling frost, or even a kind of magic mushroom. But the take-away for most of us is that manna is bread, and it saved the Israelites.

It also gave us the term *mannitol*. The next pill you take may have been made with mannitol, which the W.H.O., by which I don't mean the famed rock band, lists as an "essential medicine."

But bread is also spiritual food, no doubt about it: The doctrine *transubstantiation* says the bread and wine on the Lord's table are not symbolic but the actual substance—body and blood—of Christ. The *Showbread* offered to God at the Temple table (baked in a secret, sacred process by the Garmu family) is described in the Talmud and also by the first-century historian Josephus (born Joseph ben Matityahu), who gives details of the Temple's layout and who's also the sole witness to the historical Jesus.

Another Joseph is Saint Joseph the Provider ("Joe the Pro"). The name *Joseph* means "he who increases." This is the man who keeps bread on our tables. As Jesus's father, he's the *paterfamilias*, head of the household. He handles all domestic affairs, which is why you bury his statue in the yard to help sell your house. Bury him upside down, facing the house, near the For Sale sign. To seal the deal, have faith "in yourself, in your Sale and in Saint Joseph." (If you live in a condo, bury the figurine in a pot. *Condo*—short for *condominium*—means "housing together.")

For the Feast of Unleavened Bread at Christ's Last Supper, there were thirteen at the table, which makes thirteen an unlucky number—and taken seriously, too, as in buildings without a floor numbered 13. Add that the Crucifixion was said to occur on a Friday, and Friday the 13th is a day to just not even get out of bed. I bet you anything there was some *Twilight Zone* episode about a 13th floor, or at least about Friday the 13th. (*Twilight*, incidentally, is the moment where there are "two-lights.")

The unleavened bread (matzo) eaten during Passover represents the bread the Israelites ate in the Exodus. In their hasty getaway, they couldn't hang around while it rose. *Leavened, elevate, alleviate,* and *levity* refer to rising or lifting—whether dough, pain, or spirits.

Bread is so essential that in the thirteenth century a special law, the *Assize of Bread and Ale* (approved by the Worshipful Company of Bakers), governed the price and weight of a loaf. To avoid error, the *bakester* (modern name "Baxter") would throw in an extra measure: *a baker's dozen,* or thirteen.

Speaking of bread, Latin *gluten* is "glue," which you can make by adding water to flour. This is the same gluten pilloried these days as a dietary villain: our hunter-gatherer human bodies haven't had time to adapt to agricultural products.

Grist is grain ready for grinding. Metaphors love the milling motif. 1) *Grist for the mill:* things that can be used to advantage. 2) *The mills of God grind slowly, but they grind exceeding small:* your punishment may be late but it will be unsparing. *Mill* evolved into a generic word for factory; thus *run of the mill* means mass-produced—not distinctive. A Latin millstone is a *mola,* "grinder," and your *molars* are for grinding your food after you cut through it with your *incisors.*

But before we get to bites of food, let's get *byte* out of way. A software *byte* is eight *bits,* where one *bit* is a *binary digit,* either 0 or 1. For the moment I pass over *giga-, tera-, zetta-,* and *yotta*bytes.

If bread was the staff of life, what if you couldn't get hold of any wheat? Living in the isolated Andes, for instance, you were a locavore where locavore largely meant potatoes. The word *potato*'s root, except it's not a root but a tuber, is *papa* in the Andean Quechua language. Latin *tuber* means "swelling," as in tuberculosis (*-ul* again—small lung nodes). The suffix *-osis* = an unhealthy condition, whereas *-itis* is closer to inflammation.

Sir Walter Raleigh introduced the potato to Ireland in 1589, where it eventually became the staple food. A godsend more cultivable than manna. The Irishman owned very little land, but a small plot of soil could sustain potatoes. The potato also permitted Veep Dan Quayle to put his pota*toe* and his foot in his mouth simultaneously.

Speaking of which, in 2003, in the most puerile political notion in history, Bob Ney, chairman of the Committee on House Administration, whatever that might be, so deplored France's opposition to the invasion of Iraq that he rechristened "French fries" *freedom fries*. What a bozo. Only an opinion. Then there's the article from WWI warning citizens about sauerkraut: "Don't lay yourself open to the charge of pro-German-ism hereafter by calling it 'sauerkraut': Refer to it as 'Liberty Cabbage.'" The article's catchy conclusion: "BUY, BUY LIBERTY CABBAGE! AND BYE-BYE SAUERKRAUT!"

And what of *spud*? It's (possibly) derived from the *spade* (etymological kin to *spoon*) that dug it up.

The British don't have French fries; they call them *chips*. They've found their own ways, though, to diss the French. A condom? A *French letter*. Unauthorized absence? *French leave*. Syphilis? The *French disease*—though the Neapolitans used that phrase first. Of course, the French are traditionally connois-seurs of romantic (and sexual) love. An *affaire de coeur* is usu-ally also an affaire de *corps*. By the way, what we now call an STD used to be *VD*: venereal (Venus's) disease.

As for the unlovely STD *crabs*, it is named for tiny crab-shaped parasites. The crab is the symbol for cancer, named by an early Greek for the shape of a breast tumor. You find the Crab among the Zodiac animals circling the sky. *Zodiac* and, of course, *zoo* derive from *zo*, which is the Greek root of *zoology*, *zoa* (valuable in Scrabble), and *Neoprotoozoic* (the new early-animals era), *etc.*

Returning to the Americas, *avocado* evolved from the Aztec Nahuatl word *ahuacatl* ("testicle") into Spanish *aguacate*. (Likewise, *huacamolli* became "guacamole.") *Testicle* is visually good, but so is the avocado's other name, *alligator pear*, which it owes to a non-Spanish speaker who misheard "avocado" as "alligator."

In the produce department, another interlingual error resulted in the *Jerusalem artichoke*. This unsightly but edible tuber, which makes a potato look like a prom queen, belongs to the sunflower family (Italian *girasole*—"turning to the sun"). When one greengrocer hawked his *girasoles*, a buyer understood *Jerusalem* and created a brand new word.

The Nahua language gave us another pair of indispensable foods—*chocolate* and *tomato*. Strangely, the *cacahuatl* (cocoa tree) belongs to the *Sterculiaceae* family, named after Sterculius, the Roman god of feces (note: *cacahuatl* is unrelated to our *caca*). From the tree's beans the Aztec made *xocolatl*, "bitter water." In 1502, Columbus took the first cacao beans back to Spain, but nobody noticed—until 1528, when the Conquistador Fernando Cortés realized he was onto something with this new Nahua brew. Someone had the idea of adding sugar, and botanists called it *Theobroma cacao*, "God's food."

By the way: Columbus's cocoa didn't catch on, but we do have him to thank for *cannibals*. The *Caribbean* tribes called themselves *caribals*; Columbus heard *canibals*, which he took as evidence he'd indeed arrived in the land of the *Khan*.

Anyway, that's chocolate. *Vanilla* derives from Latin *vagina*, Latin for "sheath" (like the vanilla-bean pod). In the Aeneid, for example, the Romans are always putting their swords in their *vagina*s.

The tomato, *tomatl* in Nahua, was first cultivated by the Aztec. The tomato is a fruit (to settle that question) which the Italians called *pomodoro*, "apple of gold." Like the potato, the tomato was a mega-hit with the Old World.

Idioms about fruit are often positive. A *plum* job is a sought-after one; the (British) upper-classes speak with a *plummy* accent. Life's a *bowl of cherries*. *Apple-cheeked* refers to rosy cheeks, not mumps-chic. A *peaches-and-cream* complexion is warm-hued. *Cream*, by the way, is an etymo-cousin of *Christ*: their common ancestor is Greek *khrisma*, "oil." *Christ* is the "anointed one."

Orange descends from Arabic *nāranj*, which had to pass through Old French *pomme d'orenge* ("an orange-tree apple") to get into English.

You do, however, run into downbeat fruit. People *go bananas*. A *lemon* is a car that craps out on you. A *prune* is a sourpuss. *Sour grapes* = resentment. A *bad apple* spoils its neighbors. To *peach* on someone is to rat them out. A messed-up situation is one that *went pear-shaped*.

The fruit object that takes the cake, though, is the fruitcake, which is not something you strive to be described as. Take the Christmas fruitcake: active ingredient, candied fruit, but a bottle of syrup of ipecac would be more welcome. The fruitcake is a weighty confection, permeated with liquor, with a use-by date counted in years if not decades. This object doesn't justify its footprint on any shelf and is customarily jettisoned, or regifted as a joke.

Ipecac (preceding paragraph) is the Brazilian plant *ipe-kaaguéne*: "small-leaves-vomit." We're supposed to keep it in our medicine cabinets in case we ingest poison. Thanks, Brazil. But Brazil also gave us the *cashew* nut, *acajú*, verbal cousin to the *pistachio*.

A *pomegranate* is a "many-seeded apple" (*granum* = "grain"). It was a bad day for Persephone when Hades fed her the magic pomegranate seeds that brought her to the Underworld every fall. But maybe, like winter vacationers who seek the healing heat of balmy resorts (*balm* is akin to *balsam*), Persephone lounged happily in a *chaise longue* on the banks of the fiery Hadean river, Phlegethon. And please do not say "chaise *lounge.*" A chaise *longue* is a *long* chair, one you can stretch out your legs on.

Lord Hades himself, however, did *not* warm *the cockles of her heart*, i.e., her *cochleae cordis* (cardiac cavities). The *cochlea* is a snail shell, like the cockles whose shape gave us the cochlea in our ears. (By the way, be aware that the Old English noun *shape* once connoted "female genitalia": the idea of giving birth broadened into the idea of creation in general and hence the concept "to shape," in the sense of forming or creating something.)

The *pineapple* is an apple that looks like a pinecone but Brobdingnagian (a giant resident of Brobdingnag, where Gulliver washed up in his travels). This fruit became a symbol of hospitality: in colonial America a host would offer a pineapple to guests who'd survived a long sea voyage but had developed *scurvy* (a corruption of Latin *scorbutus*) from lack of ascorbic acid—vitamin C.

Incidentally, the party *piñata* also gets its name from its original pinecone shape.

Cockney rhyming slang is a fan of fruit. *Apples and pears* = "stairs." *Raspberry tart* = "fart" (if you "give someone the raspberry," you blow a rude noise through your lips). It's worth noting that the Romani language has two words for fart, one for the sound, the other for the scent. When naming a brand, by the way, be sure it doesn't mean "fart" in some Scandinavian language, like one product I almost marketed. An object that did slip through corporate screening was the Chevy *Nova* that told Spanish-speakers: "It doesn't go."

Regarding bodily-cavity sounds: a Greek *poppysma* is, onomatopoetically, a lip-smacking. It can also refer to tongue-clucking, like the sound once written as *tut-tut* or *tsk-tsk*, or sometimes *tchah* or even *pshaw*, and before you say these renderings are nothing like tongue-clicking, *you* try to express it in writing. Or use a Khoisan language with the character *!* or *ǂ* to represent the sound.

But back to the raspberry tart. We get the term *dessert* (the one with two *s*'s) from the French *desservir*, as in un-serve: to clear the table. A *desert*, on the other hand, is a cognate of *series*, where *serere* means "to join together." Counterintuitive, but the concept is that a *des*ert is *un*connected to other places.

Sweet Talk. So, dessert. A *biscuit* (the British term for the American *cookie*) and a *Zweiback* are "twice-cooked" to harden them beyond breadliness.

Another hand-held is the *éclair* ("lightning"-shaped). French pâtissiers cooked up the *madeleine*, a puffy cookie celebrated for the famous *petite madeleine* that causes a sensory flashback in Proust's *Remembrance of Things Past*. In French, the *Madeleine* is Mary Magdalene, a native of the town Magdala. If you're *maudlin*, you're weepy, like Mary Magdalene. If you're a *magdalen*, you're an ex-prostitute like the one whose seven demons Jesus deactivated.

Gingerbread derives from Latin *zingiberi*, echoing Zanzibar (now part of Tanzania).

As Stay Puft will tell you, it was the roots of the mallow, a salt-marsh plant, that provided the main ingredient of the original *marshmallow*. One shudders to think what it must be made of today.

Getting into glop, *custard* was *croutarde*, "crusted thing." A *soufflé* is something "blown into" with air. *Mousse* = "foam." *Sherbet* is based on "syrup." *Tiramisu* means "pull me up," never mind that it's more likely to lay you low.

One non-sweet American staple is what you might call The Sandwich of Many Names: 1) *hoagie*, origin disputed and unappetizing; 2) *grinder* (same); 3) *sub*, submarine shaped; and 4) *hero*, which, according to me, and I have my opponents, began as the Greek *gyro*—originally meat roasted while turning on a spit.

Talking in Circles—a few paragraphs as a *gyro* spin-off. When a French town installs a sculpture in the center of a *roundabout* (or "traffic circle" or "rotary"), they call it *art giratoire*. And then there's Yeats's famous falcon turning in a "widening gyre"—the poem that ends on the jolly question *And what rough beast, its hour come round at last,/Slouches towards Bethlehem to be born?* The Wise Men found the answer in an *Epiphany,* from Greek *epiphainein,* "reveal."

Speaking of epiphanies, the sophisticate responds to one not with *Ha!* but with *Eureka!,* which is what Archimedes shrieked when he lowered himself into the bathtub and realized that the volume of water his body displaced equaled the volume of his submerged body.

Now I don't know about you, but I'm not sure I see this discovery as a real jaw-dropper. But I've probably misremembered (by which I mean misunderstood) it. Anyhow, *Eureka* is Greek for "I've found it"—also the root of *heuristics,* which roughly means problem-solving by trial and error.

Okay, I threw my little barb at Archimedes; but, if I understand it correctly, the bath breakthrough did lead to a piece of detective work involving *specific gravity* and other tricky things. As a student I stopped at Calculus I, stumbling around the area under a curve, which brings us full circle to circles.

Here's the place for *pi*—again not a dessert—as per Euler (say "oiler"), which is short for *periphereia,* "circumference."

More arithmetymology: The trigonometry function *secant* "cuts" a circle; a *section* is literally a "cutting," as in a *Caesarean section.* The more familiar term *tangent* (from Latin *tango,* "touch") just touches the circle's perimeter. In the unlikely event that you care, a third function is the *sine* (from *sinus,* a curve or hollow, as in *sinuous*). The anatomical sinus, which some of us know too well, is a hollow in the head.

Lentils (you thought I'd forgotten that this is a chapter on food) get their name from the Latin *lens,* "convex object." The French wear in their eyes not contact lenses but legumes—*lentilles de contact.* Legumes are called *pulses* in England. This kind of pulse evolved from the Latin *pultis,* a heavy porridge made from what we call legumes. From the same root, (etymological, not literal) a *poultice* is a compress—originally a squashy glob of hot legumes pressed on an ailing body part.

Nor does America agree with Europe on *corn*. *Korn* is the Germanic term for any variety of grain, not only the crop Americans call "corn." The word *corn* ultimately derives from Latin *granum*, "grain." A *kornel*, *Korn*'s diminutive, became English *kernel*.

When the English say *corn*, however, they mean an American's *wheat* ("white" grain); they call corn "maize," from Caribbean Arawak *mahiz*, which came to the U.S. via Mexico. In Scotland, meanwhile, *corn* = *oats*.

Talking Turkey. Algonquian *msickquatash* or *sohquttahhash* must take full responsibility for *succotash*, the corn/bean combo with a taste to match its ugly name, just my opinion. The same tribes gave us *squash*, from *askutasquash*, "something to eat raw." Indian corn was once called *turkey corn*, which is why we now *talk turkey*—to get down to actual details about something: turkeys figured in transactions between settlers and Indians. A male turkey's called a *tom*, like a tomcat. But the better tale is that Franklin named it after Thomas Jefferson.

Wikipedia informs me that *hominy grits* are "a type of grits made from hominy-corn that has been treated with an alkali in a process called nixtamalization with the pericarp removed." But for years you've been preoccupied by questions about *grits'* etymology. They are *corn*'s etymological cousin, and you can see a faint family resemblance in an ancient Baltic language, where a *gruda* is a lump of earth, which grits themselves faintly resemble. I've never had them, but pardon me if I say their photo actually looks like the result of an intestinal disorder.

As for other grains, I'll leave barley for later except to say that my favorite unit of measure is the *barleycorn*, which began as the length of one corn of barley (today 8½ millimeters or 1/3 inch). A related measure called the *poppyseed*, equals ¼ of a barleycorn. The lasts for British footwear are still measured in barleycorns. Our homunculus's shoes would be sized in poppyseeds.

Coming to rye, the Robert Burns song *Comin' Thro' the Rye* provided the title for the novel *The Catcher in the Rye*. One melody used for Burns's song shares a tune with *Auld Lang Syne* (Scots, "old long since"), traditionally caroled at midnight on New Year's Eve typically not by *teetotalers* (etymology debatable).

Rye may also be behind the less festive witch hunts in Salem, Massachusetts, in 1692. Most of the accused lived in wetlands where the main grain—rye—would be susceptible to mold. The ergot fungus in rye (also in LSD) can cause convulsions and hallucinations. When a patient presents with these symptoms, the perceptive physician immediately diagnoses demonic possession. One theory posits that the children who followed the Pied Piper of Hamelin suffered from ergotism (rye was a staple grain in medieval Saxony).

The oat is the dynamo of grains. Like a frisky horse, you *feel your oats*. You sow your wild ones.

Nowadays oats are touted for their dietary fiber. Etymological aside: another nutritional favorite is the non-grain *broccoli*—diminutive plural of *brocco* ("little projections" or "plant-shoot"). From the same root, *brocade* is a fabric with woven bumps. A perennially popular food in the body-is-a-sacred-temple world is *tofu* (Chinese, "rotten beans"), proof that some consumers are *masochists* (from a nineteenth-century novel by Leopold von Sacher-*Masoch*. You probably know about the *Marquis de Sade*. Both originated words that evolved from the strictly sexual into any type of cruelty).

Crunchy is an affectionately derisive description for a very health-conscious and environmentally-responsible eater—the type who favors crunchy granola.

Today's paleo-eaters, however, avoid cultivated grains. Our earliest cavemancestors were hunter/gatherers, and (as noted above) grains were added to the human diet more or less yesterday. It seems our GI tracts aren't yet evolutionarily ready for them. By the time they catch up, maybe we'll have moved on to foods made of processed plastics. *Paleo-*, "prehistoric," literally means "distant"; it has a somewhat sound-alike cousin, *tele-*, as in *telegraph* or *telekinesis*. When distance is as far as it can go, it reaches an end, and *tele-* also refers to "end." A *telomere* tells your cells when to stop dividing. *Teleological* is exactly what a language is not: directed towards an end or goal.

Agriculture brings us also to Latin *palea* (the part of grass that's chaff), which in Italian becomes *paglia*, "straw." A straw bed is a *pallet*, as distinct from the *palate* (*palatum*, "roof of the mouth") and the *palette* (from *pala*, "spade").

Strew was what you once did to *straw*. A *straw man*—a flimsy thing—is a deceptive argument evading the issue. Straw is substandard stuff, usually. I need only cite the doomed domicile of the first little pig. It's flimsy, but one thin blade too much will be the straw that breaks the camel's back, i.e., *the last straw*.

Hay is different from straw, or different *to* straw, as the British say, or where I often use the prepositionally faulty *than*, which is for comparisons only. Unlike straw, hay is food, as in *fodder*, a term mainly heard in the grim form *cannon-fodder*, where the food is human. As a critical link in the food chain, however, hay is happy stuff.

Some suggest that "heyday," the period of something's greatest success, derives from the cheery cry "hey." I suggest that's a crock. *Hayday* is about the culmination of the farmer's toil—haymaking—when the crop is in its prime and you drop everything else to *make hay while the sun shines*, since hay, once cut, rots in a wet field.

Here's what Hamlet says to his mother (rude, but she did remarry in very dubious circumstances):

> You cannot call it love, for at your age
> The hey-day in the blood is tame, it's humble,
> And waits upon the judgment.

While we're discussing food, and à propos of Hamlet's Denmark: I personally would blot Scandinavia off the culinary map. The staple pickled herring once nourished Norwegians through the long Nordic winter but in my opinion overstayed its welcome. On the other hand, with the Swedish *smörgåsbord* ("butter + goose + table") you at least have buffet-style options plus a handy general-purpose term for "assortment." As *bord* implies, tables were once just boards, and *board* came to mean food, as in "room and board."

In Western tradition, France is Gastronomy Central. The *chef* (from Latin *caput*, "head") is the "chief," and if you ask how *caput* became *chef,* just remember how over time a consonant can ooze from *p* to *f* without much effort. A *chef* creates master-works, aka *chef d'oeuvres* (*oeuvres*, from Latin *opus/opera,* "work"). *Hors d'oeuvres,* on the other hand, are *hors de* (outside of) the main *opus,* just as *hors de combat* means sidelined from the fray. You nibble *hors d'oeuvres* with an *apéritif,* an "opening" drink: the Gallic palate can handle the *p* in Latin *aperire* ("to open," as in *aperture*), but again *v* trumps *p* in French *ouvrir.* What we call the *entrée* once meant "introductory course"—a leftover from the era of seven-course meals.

Speaking of French food, *avalanche* derives from French *avaler,* "to swallow."

Like bacteria (below), Italian pasta is obsessed with shape. Vermicelli are "small worms." *Ziti* are "bridegrooms"—from the anatomical organ that boys, *ragazziti,* deploy on the wedding-night. *Linguine* are "little tongues." *Farfalle* (sometimes labeled "bow ties") are "butterflies." *Manicotti* are "little muffs" as in *mano,* "hand." *Penne* are "feathers/quills."

Macaroni is different, descending from Greek *macaria,* a barley liquid drunk in honor of the dead. Additional data: Yankee Doodle called his hat-decoration "macaroni" for a reason. An eighteenth-century traveler who came home flaunting Italian modes was mocked as a "macaroni." *Yankee Doodle Dandy* was a fop and a poseur: 1) Few American colonists could afford a pony. 2) The feather in his cap highlights the flamboyant dude's *panache*, another *penne* derivation. The lyricists may or may not have been using *doodle* in its "penis" sense.

His moniker "Doodle," incidentally, probably spawned the term *dude*. Less cool, a *dude ranch* lets rich urbanites pretend they are cowboys.

Another word for a fop was a *jack-a-dandy*—obsolete, but don't jettison it. It's the small reflection cast by a hand mirror, wristwatch, glass of water, etc., on the ceiling or wall.

Now to food *preparation*.

Cooking: Thanks to Latin *bulla* ("bubble"), you can *boil* a liquid or make *bouillon*. The Latin *ferveo* ("boil") also gives us *effervescent* ("fizzy") and *fervent* ("boiling"). Like *bread*, German *broth* evolved from *brewth* (above), something brewed. To *sauté* onions is to make them "jump" in the pan, like a somer*sault*. All this heating produces *steam*, whence we get *stew*. *Smoke* derives from Greek *typhus*, meaning "smoky," cognate with Latin *tufus*. Another derivitive of *tufus* is *tufa*, the rock generated from a smoking volcano. (*Lava*, incidentally, is the fiery river "washed" down from the opened vent.)

Beef? *Beef* evolved from French *boeuf*, generated from Latin *bos*, *bovis* (cow), *bovine*. But *beef* meaning "complaint" arose in the 1700s as rhyming slang. *Stop, thief!* became *Hot beef!*, which over time evolved into any kind of grievance.

Speaking of beef, a *schnitzel* is a cutlet, as in German *Schnitt*, "snip." In fact Germany wins the *wurst* award: the *hamburger*—which my mother called "Hamburg steak"—is beef "Hamburg-style." From Hamburg, go 400 miles south to Frankfurt, the home of the *frankfurter*. The city Frankfurt ("Frankish ford") arose on the Main river, a ford being a convenient spot for a city.

Etymologists speculate on the origin of *hot dog*. My own theory says that Americans named it for its resemblance to the *dachshund*, a dog bred to its skinny length to root badgers (*Dachs*) out of their burrows.

Parenthesis on *frank*: To describe the Frankish tribe who had never been enslaved, Latin created the term *francus* ("free").

Later on, Italians applied the term *lingua franca* (French tongue) to the "language" of seventeenth-century traders, which was limited to the words required to communicate business-wise with each other. The merchants' *lingua franca* was a mishmash of you name it: Turkish, Arabic, Greek, French, Spanish; it was labeled the "Frankish tongue" by Near Eastern peoples who said, "That big area in the west (aka Europe) is the 'land of the Franks.'"

The term *pidgin* was the Chinese pronunciation of "business"; it was a lingo used in commerce with Europe. A *pidgin* language has features of two languages. Sometimes a pidgin evolves further into a *creole* (cre-ole = "small created language").

Sub-parenthesis, and I know we've traveled far from food: Aspiring to a *lingua franca*, L.L. Zamenhof invented the artificial language *Esperanto* (1887). Its vocabulary smacked of words from various Western languages. Examples: "good evening" = *bonan vesperon*. "Hello" = *saluton*. *Esperanto* means "hoping," which gives you an idea of its success.

Another note on "frank": *Frankenstein* = "French stone." By the way, as you probably know, Frankenstein was not the monster but his creator.

Frankly has deteriorated badly. Meaning "free," *frank* also came to denote *speaking freely or openly*. Correct usage: *Frankly, my dear, I don't give a damn*, where Rhett Butler was revealing a candid, perhaps unwelcome, hitherto-suppressed sentiment. Going impersonal, it's now applied to facts: Frankly, Springfield's population has shrunk twenty percent in the last decade. Actual example heard last week: *Quite frankly, students were expelled.*

To return to food, head south another forty miles to Worms, which I include in the German food category because this city is famous mainly for the Diet of Worms in 1521.

No need to gag. Latin *diaeta*, "daily regimen," long ago split into two senses: 1) a "daily" food allowance and 2) the "daily" assembly of the Reichstag (literally "rule-day"). *Reich* = "kingdom"; *Österreich* (Austria), for instance, is "east kingdom." Anyway, *Worms* was originally *Borbetomagus*, Celtic for "town in a swamp." In the *b/v* swap Borbetomagus became *Vormatia*. Charles V, who headed up the Holy Roman Empire (which Voltaire called "neither holy, nor Roman, nor an empire"), hauled Martin Luther before the Diet at Worms to declare him a heretic.

Another worm fact you should know: among roundworms, *C. elegans* (*Caenorhabditis elegans*) is a VIP. He was the first many-celled organism to have his total genome sequenced. His name? "Elegant" is scientific lingo for "well-designed." Software written with efficient simplicity is "elegant."

Another term scientists like is "turn out," by which I don't mean your feet in ballet class. When revealing research results to a layperson, academics like to preface the news with "it turns out that. . . ." Here's how to use it: "It turns out the meerkat can read at a second-grade level." You'll notice this habit if you're paying attention.

Incidentally, speaking of reading: St. Augustine (fourth century) was poleaxed to see someone, namely St. Ambrose, reading—*silently*! At the time, this was not normal (or, in the single worst piece of academic lingo in the English language, normative).

But this is meant to be the culinary chapter.

Speaking Volumes. Recipes are riddled with hurdles, especially the ones you have to adjust in order to make more or fewer servings. You better know your seventh-grade *algebra*: Arabic *al-jabr*, "a reuniting." Don't confuse this with *al-Jabbar*, "the almighty," a term for Allah and the name taken by basketball great Lew Alcindor when he went Muslim and became Kareem Abdul-Jabbar.

I myself modify ingredient proportions very competently,

barring a few small snags around fractions, decimals, and division/multiplication. There's no excuse for these errors—it's not as if I need square roots or integrals or the quadratic formula. When's the last time *you* needed the quadratic formula? And I remember it verbatim, and it can't tell me where I left my car keys.

Under gastronomical math, I'll mention that *radical expressions* and the *radish* both descend from Latin *radix*—"root," which also gave us *radical* politics, which seek to *eradicate* (totally root out) contemporary ills. Aesthetically, the radish partly redeems plant roots, which I've been insulting as some of the world's ugliest items.

But back to cooking—and the enigmatic ounce: Weight? Volume? Both? These are deep waters. *Ounce* made its way to us from Latin *unus*, "one," which also evolved into *uncia*—our *inch*.

Regarding weight: a package's *net weight* specifies its contents excluding the container. *Net* = French "clear." If you *net* $10, that's what you clear after deductions.

Regarding volume: A *cubit* sounds like a measure of 3D geometry—but no. Go figure (a cliché, but apt here). It's an ancient unit of length, 45.72 cm. to be precise. Actually, it's the length of a human forearm, *cubitum*, as in Deuteronomy (*deutero* = "two," as in the isotope *deuterium*, which has a two-particle nucleus—useful in thermonuclear weapons). Examples:

> For only Og king of Bashan remained of the remnant of giants; behold, his bedstead [was] a bedstead of iron; [is] it not in Rabbath of the children of Ammon? Nine cubits [was] the length thereof, and four cubits the breadth of it, after the cubit of a man.

Another question (from the book of Matthew):

> Which of you by taking thought can add one cubit unto his stature? And why take ye thought for raiment? Consider

the lilies of the field, how they grow; they toil not, neither
do they spin . . .

Plus, of course, the specs for Noah's Ark:

The length of the ark shall be three hundred cubits, the
breadth of it fifty cubits, and the height of it thirty cubits.

Wine-bottles are measured in Biblical kings. The big sizes
start with the Jeroboam (3 litres) and progress to the Methuse-
lah, Belshazzar, Nebuchadnezzar, Goliath. Remember the historian Josephus, who gives Goliath's height as 6 feet, 9 inches (and
in the Hebrew Bible he comes in at four cubits and a span—9
feet, 9 inches, one-upping Og, emphasis on "up").

A more common container is a *pot*. *Potamos*, "river or water"
gave the Romans *potus*, a drinking cup, which turned into a
cooking *pot*. The origin of both words is Latin *potare*, "to drink,"
as in "potion" and its kin "poison."

Pot as marijuana derives specifically from the beverage
potación de guaya, guava brewed with marijuana. Marijuana =
Maria Juana, Mary Jane in English, and who knows what made
this particular girl so lucky?

A passing nod here to the acronym *POTUS*: President of the
United States, whose wife is named *FLOTUS*.

In French, *potpourri* = "rotten pot," which doesn't sound
very nice as a scent-diffuser. But *potpourri* started as a stew
made from leftovers and came to mean any mixture, as in a
combo of dried petals and spices. À propos of mixing, French
mêler, "to mix," spawned two such different terms as *mêlée* (confused brawl) and *medley*.

Is your life *going to pot*? As early as 1530, William Tyndale
wrote, of sheep, "Then goeth a part of ye little flocke to pot [i.e.,
into the cookpot] and the rest scatter."

Two celebratory *pot*-meals: *Potluck* needs no explanation
except that it's unrelated to *potlatch* from *pátlač*—a "gift" and a

"gift-giving feast" in the Chinook Jargon of the Pacific North-west. In 1884 the Canadian government banned the potlatch ceremony as a violation of "civilized [i.e., Christian] values."

A *potboiler* is a different kettle of fish and as inedible as *pulp fiction* or the *penny dreadful*. You write a potboiler not as an artistic creation but just to make a living—to have something to put on the stove and eat.

Speaking of *boil*, we all know *Boyle's Law* (V ∝ 1/V or PB = k) on temperature and gases. Boyle's name is almost as apt as "Capone."

To conclude food: A *ventriloquist* is a "stomach-speaker."

5

Buzz Words

Liquor

Every culture finds a way to make alcohol potable for everyday drinking or for a good *carouse* (from German *gar aus trinken*—"all-out drinking"). Even when it is against the law.

Certain religions forbid alcohol (and usually a few other fun things), but some alcoholic activities defy a government ban. In the seventeenth century a smuggler might hide a flask of *bootleg* liquor inside his high boot. During Prohibition, you got your booze on the quiet at a *speakeasy*, where you had to "speak softly."

In England, a *pub* ("public house") needs a license to provide booze-to-go. In America, however, a liquor store might be called a *package store*, where you can legally buy liquor only in packaged bottles.

British sailors drank the rum-blend *grog*, an allusion to the admiral's coat made of *grosgrain*—a coarse-ribbed fabric. (Another way to alleviate hurricane worries was praying to St. Elmo, patron of sailors and abdominal pain. In real life, St. Elmo was Erasmus of Formia, who continued a sermon unfazed by a near miss by a thunderbolt. If a mariner, he's your man when your mast becomes a lightning rod—the phenomenon of St. Elmo's fire, which you and I know is a "luminous fire created by a corona discharge." Don't confuse the worthy saint with Marvel's superhero St. Elmo—at 425 pounds and six feet, five inches, an unhealthy body mass index—whose specialty is transillumination, converting people into light. He dies saving the Alpha Flight team from Weapon X by absorbing the missile into himself. How I wish I could say more about this noble physicist, but duty calls me back to the bottle.)

Gin is the juniper-flavored liquor perfected by the Dutch and called *ginevra* in Italy.

Vodka means "little water": Russian *-ka* is a diminutive.

Liquor can be hot in other senses than smuggled. The term *brand* ("burning thing") gave us *brandy*, from "brandywine"—Dutch *brandewijn*; a distilled wine was a "burnt wine." American Indians called the white man's liquor *firewater*.

Wormwood (*Artemesia absinthium*) is a bitter herb and an ingredient in the liquor *absinthe*. Speaking of spirits, absinthe is nicknamed *la fée verte*, "the green fairy," for its emerald hue. Absinthe conjures up bohemians and turn-of-the-nineteenth-century Paris. Thought to be psychoactive, it was banned for a while in the US.

Speaking of colored alcohol, that's what's inside a *spirit level* (which sounds like a cheerleading parameter). A bubble within the tinted liquid shifts to show the builder whether two objects are equally high (in height, not blood-alcohol level).

Spirit has as its ancestor Latin *spirare*, "breathe." To *inspire* = "to breathe (into)." *Conspire* = "breathe together," as when you huddle and whisper. The French give us other valuable *spirits*. *Esprit de corps* is "team spirit." *Esprit* also means "wit"; less familiar but no less useful is *esprit de l'escalier*—"staircase wit": this is what galls you after you leave a dinner party and on the stairs down to the street you think of a witty remark you could have made but didn't.

Speaking of wit, English also borrows from French *bon mot* ("good word") to describe a clever comment. *Mot juste*—"the just-right word"—descends from Latin *ius*, "law, justice, or right."

To end the section we can propose a *toast*, thanks to the spice-laced toast added to wine in earlier times and left to soak, like a teabag steeping in liquid. We know that some wines are pretty mediocre, and the old days provided less choice of vintage. Some handy spice would hide the taste. Scandinavians say "*skoal*"—the "shell" they once drank from, just as the German beer *stein* was once a "stone"(ware) mug. The Old English *waes haeil* ("good health") became *wassail,* a drinking party—and we're back at the carouse that started the chapter.

6

Speaking Ill Of

Calling in Sick. Speaking of health, *health* started as "wholth"—wholeness or wellness. If you're *hale*, you're "whole" with a Scots accent. In the same pattern, *dearth* ("scarcity") adds a *-th* to the adjective *dear*—"expensive, rare." (*Dear* meaning "precious" produced "dearling": *darling.*) *Wellness* (just my opinion) is not a term used by the best people: opt for "health."

This chapter's easy to write, because today everything's an illness. If they can't shoehorn something into a disease, the fallback is a "disorder."

Medical terminology used to be enchanting. We can trace even an up-to-date hormone like *estrogen* to Latin *estrus*—a gadfly and the madness its bite produces.

The Greek *algia*, like neuralgia or analgesic, means "pain." *Nostalgia* = "home-pain."

In the past, neurological illnesses were especially prone to bizarre labels (until they were replaced by experts' surnames). *Chorea*, a symptom of Huntington's disease, was once *Saint Vitus' Dance*, from the medieval practice of dancing at the saint's shrine; Saint Vitus is the patron of epilepsy as well as dance. *Chorea* derives from "chorus," Greek for "group dancing," as in *choreography.*

Saints have their specialties. Today's health practitioners still prefer to specialize; primary care pays relatively poorly. Also, by the way, and this is odd for a man who thrives on dancing, St. Vitus is your man if you want to avoid oversleeping; he's depicted holding a rooster.

In antiquity epilepsy was known as the *Sacred Disease* (because you prayed for a cure), and later as the *Scourge of Christ* or *morbus daemonicus*, where *morbus* = "sickness," as in morbid fantasies.

The insulin that treats diabetes derives from *insula* (Latin for "island") referring to the "islets of Langerhans," which are not part of any archipelago but are cells in the pancreas. Your home *insulation*, likewise from Latin *insula*, isolates the interior from the outdoor weather: *insula* became *isola* in Italian.

Other illnesses were nicknamed unkindly. Patients with Creuzfeldt-Jakob Disorder are said to have *mad cow disease*, which was first observed in England in the 1990s and called *bovine spongiform encephalitis* (BSE). I mention elsewhere how eating parts of species closely related to yourself is a bad idea. In this case, cattle feed contained ground cow parts and caused their brains' *prions* (*prion* = Greek for "saw") to cut holes in brain tissue.

The King's Evil was the peasants' name for the disease *scrofula*. A *scrofa* was a breeding sow, prey to this illness that caused swollen lymph nodes. People thought it could be cured by the royal touch. Today, *scrofula* is known as tuberculosis. What it really is is "mycobacterial cervical lymphadenitis": *myco* is Greek "fungus," from which we get our -*mycin* antibiotics; *cervical* derives from Latin *cervix*, "neck"; *lymph* means "liquid," as in *limpid*; and *adena*- is "gland."

Fungus! should be a medical battle-cry. A *fungus* is a yeast or mold; these feed on living things. Miracle fungi are *antibiotics*, which destroy *living* bacteria. Some fungi form *spores*, the active ingredient of drugs like *Cyclosporine* ("round spore") and *Neosporin*.

Another wonderful fungus is *Penicillium*, which is shaped like a penis (Latin for "small tail"). A *penicillus* was the fine-haired tip of a paintbrush.

Bacteria are one-celled microorganisms. Like Tolstoy's line, "Each unhappy family is unhappy in its own way," they come in subgroups. Bacteria are all about shape.

One such group is the *bacilli*—"rod-shaped" (Greek *baktron* = a stick). By the way, if you ever use a topical antibiotic containing *bacitracin*, give a dose of gratitude to the patient Margaret *Treacy*, whose personal bacilli helped concoct the drug (and whose name the doctors misspelled as "*Tracy*").

Helicobacter, "spiraling rod," causes ulcers. *Campylobacter*, "bent rod," is a contagious GI infection, one of the CDC's *bêtes noires*.

Another family of bacteria is *clostridium*, "spindle-shaped." *C. botulinum* (from Latin *botulus*, "sausage") causes the paralytic disease *botulism* and also brings us Botox to paralyze the facial muscles. *C. difficile* preys on patients in whom antibiotics kill good bacteria. *C. diff* is a scourge of hospitals. This species was called *difficile* (neuter Latin adjective) because it gave scientists so much trouble to figure out.

A spherical bacterium is a *coccus* (Greek for "berry"). *Staphylococci*, for instance, resemble a *staphyle*—a bunch of grapes. The lyrically named *Staphyolococcus aureus* ("golden grapes") is responsible for pimples, impetigo, boils, carbuncles, and scalded skin syndrome.

Streptococci, "curved granules," form twisted chains. Greek *lepros*, "scaly," described *leprosy*, now called "Hansen's disease."

Greek *anthrax* (coal or charcoal, like *anthracite*) evolved in Latin into "a large boil or carbuncle." You can divine the future by *anthracomancy*, inspecting live coals, maybe more available than the pearls required for *margaritomancy*. *Typhus* means "smoky, hazy," as we saw above.

Like helicobacter, *spirochetes* come in spirals. It is here that we find *syphilis*.

The shepherd Syphilis starred in the sixteenth-century Latin poem *Syphilis sive Morbidus Gallicus*, i.e., "Syphilis, or the French Disease." To punish this youth for defiance, Apollo struck him with the spirochete we call *Treponema pallidum*: "pale thread."

The spirochete clan includes Lyme disease, which looks like a drill bit, and *leptospira*, a "thin coil." *Lepto* = "slender" (*leptins* are satiety hormones, which researchers hope to harness as a weight-loss aid). My favorite *lepto* strain is *L. interrogans*, which under a microscope looks like a question mark.

You'll notice coils and spirals seem to be very popular. My research dug up the paper "Bacterial Morphology: Why Have Different Shapes?" where we read that "cells with spiral morphologies appear to move through viscous fluids much more efficiently," and I say to them, if that's your goal, knock yourself out. Maybe they work like a propeller—sailors call a ship's propeller a *screw*.

Viruses (Latin *virus*, "potent venom") also occur in characteristic shapes: Everyone knows the *coronavirus* (COVID-19) that brought the world to a halt in 2020 is "crown-shaped." The disease's logo is an orb sprouting red crowns that look more like broccoli florets. Ebola resembles a thread: It's a *filovirus* (as in "filament" or "file," in the "single-file, please" sense of the word).

I'll wrap up diseases with *cholera*—full name, *Vibrio cholera*, because the cell's flagella make it seem to vibrate (a *flagellum* = a whip, as in self-flagellation). Greek *chol* = "bile" (or gall), a bitter fluid; hence *to gall* is "to irritate." By the Roman era, *choler* had evolved into any GI upset, while in the Middle Ages, bile was associated with a quick temper.

The ancient Greeks pretty much explained people in terms of the *four humors*—the basic fluids in the human body. They mapped the humors to the earth's fundamental elements. Each element goes with a personality type. Skip the Myers-Briggs personality test. Find a lab to analyze your humors and an endocrinologist to regulate them.

Choler (yellow bile), which made you prone to anger, was related to fire. *Melancholia* (black bile) was the earth element. *Sanguis* (blood), the air element, gave you a sanguine or optimistic outlook, not to be confused with "sanguinary," gory. *Phlegm* (some kind of cold wet transparent bodily fluid), the water element, caused apathy; in short, you were *phlegmatic*.

So, you say, speak to us of that river *Phlegethon* where Persephone wintered. Greek cartographers left us a precise geography (*geo* = "earth") of the underworld, which boasts five other rivers, including the *Lethe*, river of forgetfulness. Lethe flowed lethargically around *Hypnos'* cave, landscaped with opium poppies and inspiring Scotsman James Braid, who coined the term *hypnosis*. Our dreams issue from this cave's two exits. An ivory gate sends dreams that come true, unlike those from the gate made of horn.

Gall and personality bring us directly to Franz Joseph Gall, born in 1758 and educated in Vienna. Gall invented *phrenology*. Greek *phren* = "mind": *phrenetic* evolved into *frantic* and *frenzy*. Gall *divined* (a verb from Latin *divus*, "god") your character by palpating your cranium and measuring the relative size of twenty-seven bumps associated with "mental faculties." A Gall favorite was the bump for criminal propensity; prisons and reform schools were keen on phrenology. In a literal sense, a phrenologist, like a police informer, could "finger" you as a criminal type, ratting you out by revealing your evil tendencies.

Another phrenic disorder was named *schizophrenia*, "split mind" (as in *schism* or *scissors*).

The term *bedlam* (chaos) reflects the stigma of mental illness. The original "Bedlam" was Bethlem Royal Hospital in London. Founded in the thirteenth century by the order of St. Mary of Bethlehem, it evolved into a psychiatry-only hospital, also known as a *lunatic asylum*: a shelter for those driven insane by moon cycles.

Speaking of bedlam, why do so many expressions about disorderliness sound alike? *Higgledy-piggledy, helter-skelter, hodge-podge, harum-scarum, hugger-mugger*—and we'll make *hanky-panky*, which evolved from *hocus-pocus*, an honorary member of the club.

I Love It When You Talk Dirty. Sorry to disappoint, but this is not the section you're hoping for. The previous section treated of illnesses; this one discusses how to avoid them.

Plenty has been said about how we treat today's kids like jeweled Fabergé eggs, when in earlier generations kids followed a program of fortifying their immune systems with the standard peck or bushel of dirt *per annum*.

Since I'm reporting on scientific research, I can say it *turns out* the old wives' tales were onto something. The occasional study now supports what I'll label *filth prophylaxis*: "what-doesn't-kill-you-makes-you-stronger."

Phylax/phylact- means prevention. You use a *prophylactic* condom. A Jewish man might wear a *phylactery*, a small leather box containing Hebrew prayers for the purpose of warding off evil. *Anaphylactic* shock, as from a bee sting, shows you lack protection from the venom.

Inoculation renders something harmless: Latin *noxa* is "harm" (think *noxious* and *obnoxious*). In the days of smallpox, you were *vaccinated* (from *vacca*, cow) with cowpox, a benign relative of smallpox. You might think *immunization* stems from Latin *munire*, "to fortify," as in *munitions*). But no. From the same root as "com*mun*ity," *immunis* once meant "exempt from taxes." Com*mun*icable diseases are taxing.

Rev up the time machine again and get off at the eighteenth century, and I don't mean into a picturesque movie set. You'll run into a lot of smallpox survivors disfigured by pockmarks. Then visit a farm and check out the beautiful skin of the dairymaids, who contracted cowpox from cows and were henceforth immune to what Edward Jenner called the Speckled Monster. In 1796, Jenner injected fluid from blisters of a dairymaid's cowpox (which she had contracted from the bovine vector Blossom) into a child. By 1800, early anti-vaxxers were depicting patients with cows' heads to protest the cowpox vaccine that would eventually whack smallpox for good.

And while you're back there, drop in on a couple of military garrisons. You'll note that smallpox incidence is lower among cavalry (who are exposed to an equine strain of pox) than among infantry.

Nowadays tots get lots of shots, not that these prevent most viruses, colds, or the calamitous GI pestilence *norovirus* from Norwalk, CT, not far from the town of Old Lyme, known since 1975 for Lyme disease. Anyway, research on filth prophylaxis says that, like cowpox, a household pet can boost your resistance to allergies and asthma, thanks to all the immunizing dander wafting around the house. Research claims dogs and cats also bring indoors microbes that help stave off colds.

Incidentally, though an antibiotic will not kill a *virus*, doctors who should know better fling them around as a kind of *placebo* that *placates* their patients. Like mold, antibiotics break down living things like bacteria, but a virus is just a bundle of DNA that can't live without a host, which is why it gloms onto a cell and mutilates and mutates it. The *flu* is a virus, short for *influenza*, Italian "influence of the stars." Don't confuse it with your chimney *flue*, or, speaking of dogs, with a dog's *flews*, pendulous upper lips that fling drool, in my Newfoundland's case, up to the actual ceiling.

But still we have Mom, phobic on phantom germs, going after her hands like Lady Macbeth with a vial of Purell. Today's parents swaddle the little larva in a safe cocoon. The post-larval *pupa*, by the way, is Latin "doll" or "small person," which also gave its name to the *pupil* of the eye, where, when looking at someone else, you see a small image of yourself.

7

Say It with Flowers

Many a flower gets even prettier if you know the origin of its name. *Pansy* = French *pensée*—"thought." *Tulip* means "turban" (*tülbent* in Turkish). A *rhododendron* is a "rose-tree," which is a bad description of those leathery fiascos. A *fiasco* is an Italian "flask." Probably our fiasco derives from an Italian custom, *fare il fiasco*, whereby the loser in a game has to pay the winner a bottle of wine.

A Rose by Any Other Name. Rose varieties like to be named for women—typically duchesses, but some are folksy: *Ann's Beautiful Daughter, Gee Whiz, Betty Boop, Julia Child.* You do get plenty of men, such as *Reichspräsident von Hindenberg.* Some sound more like race-horses: *Square Dancer, Sky's the Limit, Strike It Rich.*

Then there's the *Chrysler Imperial* tea rose—fragrant and magnificent, though lacking the car's *Full Speed Driving Collision Warning, Uconnect® Access+ and "paddle shifters" for kayak mode.*

Other flowers are bad news.

Belladonna—"beautiful lady"—is the atropine-harboring "deadly nightshade." (In a non-toxic form, your optometrist uses it to dilate your pupils.)

The *foxglove* (*Digitalis pupura*) is not a vulpine mitt. *Foxglove* = "folks' glove," where "folks" are fairies, and you better call them "good folk" or "wee folk" or there'll be consequences.

Anyway, to the fanciful, the *digitalis* leaves resemble fingers. The Scots call the foxglove flowers "dead man's bells." Like belladonna, it's a Jekyll-and-Hyde: poisonous except when it's a drug for heart disorders.

Speaking of *fox*, we'll see later that it descends from the German *fuchs*. Some claim that it was the sixteenth-century botanist Leonard Fuchs who first named the foxglove (after himself). What we do know is that the *fuchsia* flower was named in honor of Fuchs.

Flowers often come with baggage: flower myths are thick on the ground.

The fate of the youth Hyacinth, Apollo's lover, involved proto-Ultimate Frisbee, where *ultimate*, sadly, is the apt term. While the two were tossing a discus around, Hyacinth was struck and killed. Apollo's tears sowed the *hyacinth* flower.

The *narcissus* likes wet soil. A flower sprang up in the spot where the youth Narcissus was glued, admiring his reflection in the water, until he wasted away. The *lily* sprang out of pure white milk leaking from lactating Juno. *Daffodil* evolved from *asphodel*, probably for its resemblance to today's *asphodel* of the lily family, more notably the flower that grew in the Greek underworld.

Like *laundry*, *lavender* evolved from Italian *lavanderia*, "things to be washed." The plant was used as a clothes freshener. It smells better than, say, the misspelled *Downy Unstopable* with the ad that touts its "feisty freshness," unaware that *feisty* evolved from Middle English *fisten*—fart.

Artemisia honors Artemis, goddess of natural things. It's a landscaper's favorite, never mind that Moses warned the children of Israel against its "root that beareth gall and wormwood."

Many herbs are just plain lyrical. *Oregano* means "joy of the mountain." *Rosemary*, from *ros marinus*, is "dew of the sea." *Basil*, derived from *basileus* ("king" in Greek), is known in French as *l'herbe royale*: a *basilica* is a church modeled on a royal court.

By the way, in another *b/v* cognate pair, the name *Basil* is Vassily in Russian. We do the same thing with Hebrew: Devorah/Deborah. Avner/Abner. Avram/Abraham. Avigail/Abigail.

Some flowers get their labels from the botanists who studied them: *dahlia* from Swede Anders Dahl; *forsythia* from William Forsythe; *poinsettia* from Joel Poinsett, first American ambassador to Mexico. Carolus Linnaeus, the father of binomial nomenclature (genus + species), named the *zinnia* in honor of a Dr. Zinn.

From the sublime to the ridiculous with the *dandelion*. From France we adopted *dent-de-lion*, "lion's tooth." But the French also and less imposingly called it *pissenlit*, "bedwetting." (French *lit* = "bed": in English a *litter* is a "bed-full" of kittens or a first-aid stretcher.)

But where dandelions are concerned, don't let your guard down. The dandelion might mean *Danger!* Calgary, Alberta, is crusading for "dandelion containment." One resident calls slippery dandelion leaves "a threat to public safety." Another wrote: "streets go wild with weeds when we all pay our taxes for a safe environment." A "dandelion infestation threatens the long-term health of the landscape." Calgary city ordinances permit dandelions in your own personal yard (max. six inches high). Calgary law also governs other plants. A tree interfering with power lines? *Non-compliant vegetation.*

Sobering stuff.

8

Too Funny for Words

Laughter

Indeed, time for some comic relief.

Scientists have done much research into the curative powers of laughter. *What?* you say. But not so fast. Are you aware, for example, that a Vanderbilt University study has found that 10–15 minutes of laughter burns 50 calories? Or that rats laugh when you tickle them? Or that laughter yoga and laugh parties aid memory? Vitally important research, which I hope was funded privately rather than on my tax dollar (like Neanderthal man, incidentally, the *dollar* originated in the German *Thal*, "valley or dale." *Thaler* evolved into *daler*).

We inherit the onomatopoetic "laugh" from Dutch *lachen*. Not much of a sound-alike, you think, until you hear the Old English form *hlæhhan*.

Beyond Words. Laughter merits a one-page digression from etymology proper.

Studies report that we change physiologically when we laugh. For instance—and here's a real shocker—WebMD reports that "we stretch muscles throughout our face." Incredible!

Since education is the key to good health, why not become a laugh instructor? The Laughter Wellness Institute (three levels of training) invites *you* to "become a certified laughter wellness teacher" (International Certification). They throw in a starter kit and Laughter Session Planner©.

"Joyologist" Steve Wilson, M.A., C.S.P., developed a similar curriculum for health and human service professionals. The $500 fee includes an "Official Certified Laughter Leader (CLL) T-shirt plus a Certificate and Code of Ethics . . . suitable for framing," and tips on "Marketing, Setting fees, and Building repeat business." Also available: "Materials in Italian, French, Hungarian, Spanish."

Aside: Best practice, in my useless opinion, would have nixed *joyologist*, which mixes the Romance *gioia* with the Greek *-ology*. I'd prefer some such word as *geliology*. *Gelomancy*, divination by laughter, passes muster: Greek *manteia* means "divination" and brings us the *praying mantis*.

Caveat: Laughter Online University claims laughter is "usually well-tolerated," but contraindicated, especially "intense side-splitting laughter," in cases of severe angina, hemorrhoids, or incontinence.

But few have the calling to become guffaw-guides. Plus, consumers may shun your laughter-wellness course, which no sane and sober health insurance would cover.

You might consider *laughter yoga*, which "strengthens the immune system, reduces pain and lowers stress." *Yoga* derives from Hindi/Sanskrit "union," which also lets us *yoke* our oxen together.

In one mirth-origin myth, Australian spirits who wanted humans to lighten up hoisted a bright star into the heavens. Nobody noticed it except the kookaburra bird, who started letting out gonzo cachinnations—the first laughter.

Another researcher was J. M. Barrie, author of *Peter Pan* (named for the god Pan, whose *panpipes* used to spook the locals into *panic*). Barrie posits that laughter generates fairies:

> When a new baby laughs for the first time a new fairy is born . . . there are always new fairies. They live in nests

on the tops of trees; and the mauve ones are boys and the white ones are girls, and the blue ones are just little sillies who are not sure what they are.

LGBTQ might want to weigh in on the "little sillies."

They say laughter is the best medicine, but, despite the claims of "Laughter Consultant" and "laughterpreneur" Sebastian Gentry, laughter does not always "leverage wellness."

We now pass to the Tanganyika (now part of Tanzania) laughter epidemic of 1962, an outbreak of mass hysteria. *Hysteria*, deriving from "uterus" in Greek, smacks of misogyny, so let's call it by its technical name, mass psychogenic illness (MPI). This epidemic, which started with three schoolgirls, lasted eighteen months and spread to a thousand people. Besides pain and crying attacks, symptoms included *flatulence* (*inflated* gut) and random screaming.

Dancing Around the Subject. A similar strain of fun-gone-furious caused the Dancing Plague of 1518 in Strasbourg, Germany. The index case (or Patient Zero), Frau Troffea, started dancing in public and infected 400 men and women; cardiac arrest killed several of them. Doctors diagnosed the cause as "hot blood" and prescribed dancing 24/7 to get it out of their systems. The town fathers even hired bands to keep them at it.

Another sixteenth-century *choreomania* outbreak, in Taranto, Italy, was supposedly caused by the bite of a local spider, the *tarantula*. This disorder, also known as *tarantism*, has its own patron, St. Paul: the afflicted women who danced in front of St. Paul's church became "St. Paul's brides." Hence our *tarantella* dance.

Roman mythology had its own choreomaniacs. The *Bacchantes*, followers of Bacchus, drank and danced themselves into a frenzy—often violent, occasionally murderous. Referring to their mania, the Greeks called them *maenads*.

We haven't come all that far since then. In a *mosh pit* (from "mash") slam dancers push and crash into each other. At a Pearl Jam concert in 2000, eight young men suffocated in a mosh pit.

Since as usual I've strayed from laughter, I'll end with some dancing as structured as moshing is free-form. We see square dancing's European roots in moves like *do-si-do* (French *dos-à-dos*, "back-to-back"). *Allemande*, another dance term, is French for "German-style." The *polka* from Bohemia may mean "woman from Poland," or it may derive from the Czech for "half," as in half-steps. The Csárdás is Hungarian. *Flamenco* = "Flemish": the Spanish once reigned in Flanders, a fact new to me. (*Castanets*, incidentally, were made of chestnut—genus "*Castanea*"—wood.) Ballet speaks French, but some of its steps are more exotic, like *arabesques* ("Arabian-style").

The *leotard*, by the way, commemorates the trapeze acrobat Jules Léotard. More interestingly, the *tutu* comes to us from *cucu*, a toddler's pronunciation of *cul*, the ballerina's bottom that it barely conceals. (Latin *culus* = "bottom," as in *cul-de-sac*, literally "bottom of the bag.")

9

Bespoke
Clothes and Cloth

Ballet-wear prompts a look at terms for clothing, and we'll start at the feet with a word honoring the Worshipful Company of Pattenmakers. *Pattens* came from *pattes* (French, "paws"), and considering pattens' one-time importance, they've gotten too little airplay. Crucial footwear from the Middle Ages through the twentieth century, pattens were wooden platform soles without uppers. You strapped them onto your shoes to keep your feet out of barnyard dung and even raw human sewage streetside that would give us the squeams.

Laborers also wore wooden clogs, or *sabots*, which protesters allegedly tossed into factory machinery during the Industrial Revolution to *sabotage* the works. *Sabot*'s etymological cousin is *ciabatta* bread, which is shoe-shaped.

More urbanely: On the late-nineteenth-century street, you could protect your shoes from grimy splashes by wearing *spatterdashes* (*spats*) as modeled by Babar and Uncle Scrooge McDuck, though if anything can waddle contentedly through muck, a duck is it.

Speaking of urbanity, *mulleus* (Latin "red") is the source of the slippers we call *mules*. Roman senators wore *calcei mullei* to match their red-edged togas.

As for women, feet too often mean pain. From the tenth century until the 1930s, upper-class Chinese ladies underwent

55

foot binding to show they didn't do physical labor and didn't need feet that actually worked. Foot binding involved breaking the toes, sometimes infecting them so they'd drop off—an unseductive phase for the "lotus-feet" women strove for. But it wasn't only about fashion. Crippling a woman made her weak and dependent.

There have long been ladies who shunned the sun to show status, a statement that shares sounds with "she sells seashells by the seashore," which a true lady did not: a suntan was for field-workers. Not till the twentieth century did a tan show you had the money and leisure for melanoma-seeking. *Melanoma*, like *melatonin* and *melancholy*, stems from Greek "black."

Nowadays women's feet are lucky enough to have choices—stiletto heels, for example. (A *stiletto* is a small dagger, from *stylus*, "sharp point.") Wear these too often and you'll be hearing from your feet in middle age.

And let's hope Cinderella got rid of *her* flimsy footwear, which wouldn't have fit by the time pregnancies and age had spread her foot like pancake batter in a skillet (actually, contractually, the happily-ever-after clause probably prohibits aging). She could hardly give them to the buniony stepsisters, whom she probably didn't see much of anyway. I'm guessing Goodwill, or she used them to hold hair-elastics.

À propos of princesses, the *court shoe*, formerly a low-cut opera slipper, eventually described the unpretentious (until the 1980s, anyway) tennis shoe.

We all know "Cinderella" means "little cinder-sweeper." Cinderella's cousin *Rapunzel* owes her name to the similarly humble *rapunculus*, a little Latin *rapum*, "turnip." *Rapum* is also the source of the dazzlingly-yellow *rape* plant.

I myself empathize with the ugly stepsisters. Every embryo should get attribute-parity, each inheriting total personal assets of equal value from a menu including good looks, 20-20 vision, kindness, perfect pitch (also a good throwing arm), high IQ, hips and cheeks that will never develop fleshy saddle-bags, and resistance to cavities and nose-hairs. If one fairy tosses in the gene for early-onset spindle-death, the next fairy commutes it to a century-long siesta and throws in a positive trait or two to balance things out. Grossly obese? Your IQ is astro. You're ADHD? You're also MVP.

Parenthesis: *IQ* is the "intelligence quotient" you get when you divide mental performance by age, and see what happens to that quotient as the denominator increases. Meanwhile, if your intelligence ranks in the top 2%, you can join *Mensa*, which is Latin for "table." The website describes it as "a round-table society"; the same concept as King Arthur's Round Table where no one knight had a seat more prominent than another. (From *mensa*, by the way, the Spanish derived *mesa*, "plateau, tableland.") How delightful, especially for us sub-Mensa dunces, that *mensa* in Spanish actually means "stupid, silly."

Rapunzel's not the only girl famous for her long hair: Lady Godiva lived in the eleventh century, and her actual name was something like *Godgifu* ("God's gift"). She ordered the locals to stay away while she rode around town naked, with only her hair to cloak herself. (The original *Peeping Tom*, supposedly, was a man who disobeyed her.) She wasn't a mere flasher, however; the stunt was a protest against high taxes.

That's Godiva. There were many women at the time with similar Anglo-Saxon forenames, but not all of the names were Christian. Take *Aelfgiva* (or Aelfgifu), "gift of the elves." Aelfgyva makes a cameo appearance in one panel of the *Bayeux Tapestry*, which is an embroidered storyboard of the Norman Conquest. The caption reads: "A certain cleric and Aelfgyva—," leaving the verb to our probably prurient imagination.

How did we get here? This chapter was an examination of clothes.

Today dress codes *barely* exist: I give you the thong *bikini* (named for the Bikini Atoll, an atom-bomb test site). A laudable trend.

The stresslessness of being able to go anywhere in anything! Neckties evaporate. Bra straps show. The once *de rigueur* (rigorously required) daily shave goes optional. Anything goes: *In olden days*, says Cole Porter, *a glimpse of stocking was looked on as something shocking*—now no more stockings, period. The repulsive word *pantyhose* will evolve its way out of the vernacular, surely leaving the vile "panty" behind. Actually I personally don't know anyone who uses the term.

Along came *casual Fridays* at work and *dress-down days* in schools. *Casual* has strayed far from the Latin "to fall," progressing from "accidental" (*casualty*)—to "irregular" (*casual* laborer)—to "non-serious" (a *casual* remark)—to "informal." The earliest meaning of *a dressing-down*, by the way, was a severe reprimand in the military, whereby you lost your rank and the insignia and stripes on your uniform.

Speaking of military dress, we get the cute term *mufti* from British colonial India: it designated civilian clothes—"civvies" to Americans. A *mufti* is a Muslim jurist who rules on religious matters (Israel's Netanyahu blamed a mufti for the Holocaust). The English evidently borrowed *mufti* to mean "authorized [to skip your uniform]," using it in a secular sense as we do *kosher*.

A "*man of the cloth*" is a clergyman. "The cloth" once referred to the uniform worn in *any* profession. Later, because a priest's robes were so conspicuous, the meaning narrowed to clerical garb.

Being out of uniform is one thing; some garb crosses the line into the *grotesque*. (Literally, *grotesque* = "grotto-dwelling," like *Cro-Magnon* man, where *cro* meant "cave" in *Catalan*.) Anyway, two tasteless (I use the word advisedly) examples of duds as food, and food as duds:

First, *Candypants*, edible underwear (1975) from the *Cosmorotics* (I'll say more later about portmanteau words) company. Our noun *candy* originated in late Middle English from French *sucre candi*, "cane sugar," based on Persian *qandī*. *Sugar* was the gift of Arabic *sukkar*, "sugar."

Secondly, Lady Gaga's dress made of raw beef. She wore this

to protest the "Don't ask, don't tell" policy. Symbolic connection of this military policy with an edible dress?—am I missing something? Whatever, the garment was then preserved as dried meat. If she falls on hard times, Lady Gaga, can throw away the dress's hem-edging (untrimmed fat) and eat it like giant jerky. More gag than Gaga.

Despite their aristocratic titles, "Lady" Godiva and "Lady" Gaga, both made political statements on behalf of the common man using apparel.

Well, *de gustibus non disputandum est* (there's no arguing about tastes). A Gallic *gastronome* (stomach-connoisseur) would agree: *chacun à son goût* (each to his own taste).

By the way, Gaga's meat-outfit probably wasn't off the rack but made to order, or *bespoke*—the past participle of the old verb "bespeak."

They say *il faut souffrir pour être belle*, by which they mean, "Beauty has always had its costs," such as:

◗ Corsets that halved lung volume and often caused fainting. And think of the heartburn.

◗ Minor and major cosmetic surgery that damages if not you at least your bank account.

◗ A common procedure, literally for the birds, can delete your *crow's feet*—goose feet in French; rooster feet in Spanish; hen's feet in Italian. The Greeks, Germans, and Swedes are solid with us Anglophones on crows: *korákia pódia*, *Krähenfüss*, and *kråkfötte*, respectively. Crow's feet in Polish are *bazgroly*, "scribbles." In Chinese, less imaginatively, 眼角的) 魚尾紋 means: "eye-wrinkles."

◗ Speaking of beauty taking a toll, an advertisement claims you can fix your wrinkles the way the DPW fixes highways, with "skin resurfacing."

◗ "Brush-rollers" were hair curlers cunningly engineered to perforate the scalp with stiff quills while a girl tried to sleep.

❧ A *blowout* en route to work used to mean a flat tire. Today
it's hair: a stop at a blow-dry bar, which—with a price range
of $15–$400—I call suffering, feel free to disagree; anyway,
it's no "blow-out sale."

Speaking of hair, the language *Hindi* ("beyond the Indus
river") gave us *shampoo*: *champo* = scalp-massage.

Talk a Blue Streak. *Denim* has undergone many abuses: ready-
made fraying and holes, pre-faded groin-wrinkles (sometimes
even artificially dirty). Time was, blue-jeans came in a magnificent over-dyed indigo blue. Calculate their color saturation to
see how they surpass today's lame article:

$$S_{ab} = C^*_{ab}$$

Lame is the word. Real denim is so stiff that new jeans used
to almost stand up by themselves. Fading and softening over
time were earned notches in the wearer's belt. I'd call pre-dis-
tressed jeans cheating—if they fooled anyone. As it is, they're
merely ghastly.

Second prize for denim-perversion: denim decorated with
other material. Denim with leopard-skin accents, for instance.

You thought denim was created by Levi Strauss during the
Gold Rush. No. The world's most popular attire reflects *two*
southern European cities.

One: the word *denim* started as "French silk"—*serge de Nîmes,*
where Nîmes is a city in southern France, visited for its well-
preserved Roman sites. *Serge* is a silk fabric, from Latin *sericus*
"silk." (And let's not forget the Spanish adage, *A monkey dressed
in silk is still a monkey.* Add to that *You can't make a silk purse
out of a sow's ear.*)

Two: *jean* was a twill fabric made in *Gênes* (French for Genoa,
better known as the birthplace of Christopher Columbus).

Genoa was a major port of call for merchants. In 1347 a
dozen ships from its harbor took the bubonic plague to Sicily,
whence the Black Death spread to decimate Europe's popula-

tion, though to *decimate* is to destroy only one *tenth*; and the plague wiped out closer to one third. To cover the plague's incubation period, Italy made foreign ships wait offshore for forty (*quaranta*) days. The French called this period a *quarantaine*, which became our *quarantine* (see *corn teen*, below). In 2020 *quarantine* became a term used far too frequently.

Columbus never quite made it to North America, but he contributed his name to Washington, where D.C. = District of Columbia. We all know it was Amerigo Vespucci who would give *America* its name, even if that's about all I know about him.

Sub-detour: *Columbus* means "dove," a fancy term for pigeon—the bird who alerted another sailor, Noah, that he was nearing land. In a cemetery you'll find a *columbarium* (Latin "pigeon-house"): a repository for ashes. Façade-wise, it looks like a grid of post-office boxes or safe-deposit boxes, or a Rubik's Cube but less colorful.

An Italian *catches two pigeons with one bean*. Gentler than *killing two birds with one stone*, though it still ends badly for the birds.

In a happier vein: in 1945, the pigeon Mary of Exeter was awarded the *Dickin Medal for Animal Valor* for "conspicuous gallantry and devotion to duty whilst serving with British Empire armed forces." Assaulted by gunshot, shrapnel, and a German fighting hawk, Mary just carried on flying messages between England and France.

Noah's dove carried an olive branch, an early Greek and Roman symbol of peace. It was Noah's son Shem, by the way, who begot the *Shemites* (*Semites*). Speaking of which, Semitic-language cognates for "peace" include *Salem*, *Shalom*, and the name *Absalom*. Derived from Hebrew S_L_M, these are cousins of the Arabic *salaam*, which came from *Islam*, "submission."

Since pacifists are known as *doves*, you might guess that the peace symbol ☮ represents a bird in flight. Incorrect. In 1958, Gerald Holtom designed the modern peace symbol by combining the semaphore signals for *N* and *D* ("nuclear disarmament").

Semaphore = Greek "sign-carrier," and the system of arm positions conveying an alphabetic code makes for a more delightful world. Computer languages use another kind of semaphore, best avoided by laypersons. From the same root is *semiotics*, the study of language/signs in a culture, which I mention so that I'll remember this for as long as it takes to write this sentence. We usually spell the Greek stem not *-phore* but *pher*: a *pheromone* "carries" an attractive odor; *Christopher* = "Christ-bearer."

In English we carry things not with a *ph* but an *f* (*aquifer*, *transfer*); the Romans had no letter *phi*, but they had a perfectly serviceable *f*. Speaking of Greek and Latin, I'm forever gushing about the greatness of the English language given its Germanic *and* Classical roots—but there's more! Split the Classical sector further, into Latin *and* Greek alternatives (like *multi-colored* and *polychromatic*), and you start to really up the word count.

But I've gotten a long way from denim—which now takes us to *pants*: The word stems from Greek *panteleemon*, "all-compassionate" (another Greek term is *eleemosynary*, "charitable"). *Saint Pantaleon* was one of the *Holy Unmercenaries*, who accepted no payment for their good deeds. It's at St. Pantaleemon Cemetery on the island Lesbos that dead Syrian refugees were buried in 2015.

Three parentheses:

1) On charitable giving: a *tithe* was the one "tenth" of your income you once had to give your church.
2) Speaking of Syria, the Eastern Mediterranean countries are known as the *Levant*, French for "rising." This rising is not the Arab Spring but the direction of the sunrise. Another "rising/east" word is Latin *orient*.
3) A *Lesbos* dweller, the poet Sappho (sixth century B.C.E.), gave *lesbians* their name.

Returning to pants—stay with me here—St. Pantaleon is a poster-child for martyrs. He was burnt by torches, then put into a pot of molten lead. When Christ cooled these instruments, Pantaleon was flung into the sea. Luckily, the stones meant to weigh him down floated. His persecutors, foiled again, hurled him to wild beasts; but he blessed the creatures and they slunk away. So he was bound to a wheel—a routine torture. But his bonds broke. When they tried to cut off his head, the sword buckled. Finally his torturers buckled, too. "If you can't lick 'em, join 'em," they said. And Pantaleon's prayers obtained their absolution.

Despite the noble meaning of his name, "all lion," the later Venetians made Saint Pantaleon into a *commedia dell'arte* stock character—an old man dressed in tight long pants. Ankle-length trousers, rivaling the then-fashionable knee-breeches, were called *pantaloons* after Pantaleon. (An aside, nothing to do with pants: the verb "to pant" started with Greek *phantasia* and reached English via French *pantaisier*, "to gasp," as at a *phantom*.)

By the way: As my sister said, "*Slacks* is not a word in one's vocabulary." Worse still, my husband uses *pant* in the singular— "It's a nice pant for casual wear." I give him a pass only because he was in the *rag trade*, better known as the garment industry.

Pants are "trousers" in the UK, where *pants* means "underpants" and where you keep your trousers up with "braces," not "suspenders." In the US you might not keep them up at all, like some young men for whom the sub-buttock waistband works, when it does, via the invisible hand of St. Pantaleon.

Some fashion analysts say this sag look began with beltless pants in prison. Others point out that looseness around the leg leaves room to conceal weapons. Whatever, the style provides street cred in a demographic not really at high risk for being viewed as *pantywaists* (effeminate sissies).

Speaking of buttocks, the *bum's rush* is not the seat of a caned chair but the ejection of an undesirable individual from a—usually public—place.

Again, you won't hear the word *panties* on my lips. One

workaround is *knickers*—women's underpants in Britain, where the word *panty* doesn't exist, which is all the proof I need that England is indeed the "other Eden, demi-paradise" described by Shakespeare in *Richard II*. Additional evidence of heavenliness: the UK lingerie store Other Eden offers an "Obsessive Police Chemise Costume."

Most think the source of *knickers* is the surname *Knicker-bocker* (from the Dutch *knickerbakker*, "baker of children's marbles"). New York society people in the nineteenth century were known as *Knickerbockers*. It was members of the elite Knicker-bocker Club who devised the game *base ball*. But the Knicker-bockers wore long pants (blue wool); it was the Cincinnati Reds who launched the knee-breeches look.

And now the Knicks are basketball. Such is evolution.

Anyhow, I claim *knickers* derives from *knee* (from Dutch *knie*), as in knee-breeches.

The knickers worn for shooting and golfing are called *plus-fours*; they droop four flaccid inches below the kneeband for freer movement, like old-style baseball uniforms. But to return to knickers as underwear, Dr. Samuel Johnson, and I'm with him all the way, wore only plant-based material next to his skin: cotton and linen. Leather or wool would be to Johnson a hair shirt, and I'd like to hear him on polyester. "Shirt," incidentally gave us *skirt*.

(Johnson may possibly be better known for publishing (in 1775, after nine years of work) a major English dictionary. *Lexicographers*, "word-writers," come in two types—*prescriptive* or *descriptive*. A dictionary like Johnson's *prescribes* correct usage. Many modern dictionaries *describe* prevailing usages without telling you how to speak.)

Luckily for Johnson, flax for linen grew in handy Holland, Belgium, and northern France. Less conveniently, raw cotton had to be imported from India, Egypt, or North America. With plenty of cheap sheep in England (and New England), wool was an easier option if the underwearer wasn't fussy.

We won't leave women's undergear without paying (non-etymological) homage to Frederick's of Hollywood, which tragically closed its stores in 2013. Since 1946, Frederick's had been the gold-standard purveyor of racy lingerie such as Naughty Knickers and a "caged bra for a jaw-dropping reception." Sad that magnificent objects such as these were often confined to a lady's *boudoir* (which means "pouting-place," and how great to have a room dedicated to sulking).

We pass over the over-revealing *camel toe* feature of tight pants. What I will say about camels is that the ancient Greeks, lacking in safari-savvy, called the giraffe a *camelopard*, a "camel-leopard." To the Anglo-Saxons the camel was an *olfend* ("elephant"). The double-humped Bactrian camel has shorter legs than the one-humped *dromedary*—from Greek *dromos* ("racetrack") as in *Astrodrome*. As also in *palindrome*, which means "running backward" (recall *paleo* = "far back"). In a *syndrome*, symptoms "run together."

A glimpse of stocking—shocking? Today's women don't know Cole Porter from Old King Cole. But they know legs. And women's legs are big business.

Ideally, a woman's legs conform to the *three-diamond rule*—the shape, not the gem. (As a shape, the diamond derives from the facets of the gem. The word *diamond* is related to *adamant*, "unyielding.") For clarity let's call it the *three-rhombus rule*. A *rhombus* (Greek) is "a sorcerer's spinning top." Anyway, when standing, you should have three vertical diamond-shaped gaps between your closed legs.

Say you're a few diamonds shy. Some brief remarks on ad-speak: Rebecca McCrensky, owner of the store Altar Ego, recommends starting with a "gateway legging in a black-based print." Altar Ego's mission: "We believe in . . . stepping outside the norms through art, laughing out loud through witty banter and combining these elements to bring a multi-dimensional experience to you through high quality self-expressive apparel." Logo: a red-and-white skull. Truly aspirational, leg-wise.

I hope this lofty goal boosts sales, because another fashion *pundit* (from Sanskrit *pandita*, "learned") laments that many printed leggings "have horrible hanger appeal."

What with the skull logo, there's a sacrificial *je ne sais quoi* about the name *Altar* [*sic*] *Ego*. An *altar* is a "high place," like altitude. An *altEr ego* is one's "other self." *Sic*, by the way, as in "[*sic*]" = Latin "thus," which is what Booth said as he murdered Lincoln: *Sic semper tyrannis*.

Let's skip with a shudder the portmanteau word *jeggings*, *leggings* spliced onto *jeans*. Designed as a win-win, it's a lose-lose, sonically if nothing else.

With legs, bare means care. Some grooming procedures involve a certain amount of *trauma* (which is the Greek word that gave us "dream," and YouTube will give you Chopin's dreamy *Liebestraum*, "love's dream"). Waxing (Old English *weax*, "beeswax") is one method, as is hair-by-hair removal via electrolysis (*lysis* = to break down, like *analysis*).

Old-fashioned shaving still works. To get really old-fashioned, in fact, consider the celebrated theory known as Occam's Razor. William of Occam was no barber, of course; as a thirteenth-century friar/philosopher, he came up with his famous principle: "Entities should not be multiplied more than necessary." They say it has to do with choosing the simplest option. I personally, however, don't know what he was talking about, but possibly it is what most men think of while shaving.

Speaking of shaving, your *mustache* grew out of the Latin *mastax*, "jaw."

But back to clothing: onward and upward with the *torso*, which "twists" at the hips (*torsion*, *contort*, *torture* share the same root). While we're on *hip* in the sense of "cool," it evolved from *hep*, meaning "with it," which was probably from West African *hepicat*, "in the know."

Now we ruminate on your arms, which sprout from your torso. To *ruminate* is to "chew on." A cow's *rumen* is a staging area whither, when she chews her cud, she brings back up a wad of fodder. She then re-swallows it into her *omasum*, also called her *bible* or *psalterium* because of its page-like folds—a religious tract right there in her GI tract.

Arm-idiom: *Give him a finger and he takes an arm* is the Italian version of our inch/mile expression.

Arm fact: One of the most appealing *midrashim* tells how Pharaoh's daughter was able to grab Moses' basket in the Nile bulrushes when her arm suddenly and obligingly extended beyond its normal length.

Arm length: an *ell* of fabric is a measure; the length from the human *elbow* to the fingertip—the same length as the cubit discussed above.

Jacket probably reaches us after a long journey from the Arabic *shakk* ("breastplate"); the Moors brought it to Spain, where it evolved into *jaco*. As for the more interesting *peacoat*, the Navy claims the *pea* stands for the initial *p* of "pilot jacket." Others go with the Dutch *pijjakker*, where *pij* meant a rough blue wool.

Not all jackets are for wearing. Another military instance is the *full metal jacket*, which describes not a uniform but a bullet. In England, you eat your baked potatoes in their *jackets*; in America, in their skins.

A thing you put your arms through is a *bra*, short for *brassière*—"braZEER," as the French do not pronounce it. A *brassière* was originally a sleeveless bodice; French *bras* ("arm") stems from Greek *brachion* and Latin *bracchia*. The word allows monkeys to *brachiate*, swinging by their arms from *branches* (which are the arms of trees). We wear *bracelets*. We *embrace*. A *brace* of something is two of it—one carried in each arm.

Another disservice to French is our "lawnjuRAY" for *lingerie* ("linens"). Our pronunciation, so similar to "laundry," is a *travesty*—literal meaning "ridiculous clothing." Before washing machines, the only clothing people used to change daily (or occasionally) was their *linen*—by which they meant underwear, collars, and cuffs. Personal hygiene was different in those days:

for nastiness, a washerwoman's in-box outranked the Augean stable which hadn't been mucked out for years. Hercules, doing some janitorial work, redirected the Alpheus River through Augeus's barn. Hercules had washboard abs, while the laundress had only a washboard.

The source of much of today's clothing is neither animal nor vegetable but mineral. *Synthetic* means "put together" (manmade out of chemical raw materials that are not household words):

$$\left[\ \overset{O}{\underset{O}{\parallel}}C\!-\!\!\bigcirc\!\!-\!\overset{O}{\underset{O}{\parallel}}C\!-\!O\!-\!(CH_2)_3\ \right]_n$$

That's polyester: purified terephthalic acid (PTA) or its dimethyl ester dimethyl terephthalate (DMT) and monoethylene glycol (MEG).

The sour-faced German philosopher Hegel, who appears to have been weaned from his mother's breast directly onto a pickle, hatched a very specific type of synthesis with his theory of *dialectics* (Greek *dia* = "apart"): one side of an argument proposes a *thesis*; the opposition states an *antithesis*; and they resolve the seeming contradiction with a *synthesis*. Think of dialectics as a *pendulum*, which means literally "a little thing that hangs but always seeks the center." Harking back to above where I say *ul* means "little." Karl Marx applied the theory to history's cycles, notably the class struggle:

a) You have capitalism.
b) A revolution wipes it out.
c) But instability is not a permanent solution; the synthesis = Communism.

Marx looks more *gemütlich* than Hegel, despite the massive black mustache paired with the white beard.

Another synthetic material, *plastic*, derives from Greek *plasma*—"substance that flows."

In the twentieth century, synthetic materials got on the *-on* suffix bandwagon: *Dacron, Nylon, Ban-Lon*—even *Rayon* which, unlike its petrochemical cousins, is mostly sawdust and cellulose. These were the products of chemistry, and if their names intentionally echo the trendy new electr*ons* and prot*ons*, give me one good reason why a synthetic textile doesn't deserve the same cachet as a subatomic particle.

Before we exit the atom: a *quantum leap* is not just any old big jump. Its concept is a *non-gradual* step, *not* on a continuum, occurring only at certain discrete levels. More like a staircase than a ramp.

But I'm not done yet with *polyester*, brought to us by DuPont, also known as the "Merchant of Death" for its status in the explosives industry. DuPont crafted plenty of unwearables such as its brand *Freon*, the freezer product notorious for making holes in the ozone layer, and the carcinogenic *Teflon*, polytetrafloroethylene, and do you really want your food cooked in that? DuPont also invented *Lycra*, a meaningless word invented out of *whole cloth* (where whole cloth is a bolt of fabric not yet cut into actual garments. Its sense is "original to the point of being a lie").

Another fabric-metaphor for a fib: a *web of lies* or a *tissue of lies*—a tale "woven" by a liar. *Web* derives from Old English for "weave," ultimately from the delightful Proto-Germanic *wabjam* (originating in *(h)uebh-*, to remind you why we shun PIE), and *tissue* is from Latin *texere*—also "weave," as in *textile*. Although none of the experts will commit to *wife*'s etymology, I posit that she derives from *weaving*, from Germanic *Weben*, as in "web."

Before it expanded into one of our most general, all-purpose words—right up there with "thing"—*stuff* used to be specifically "cloth." In its sense of *stuffing*, it started out as a quilted padding you wore under your chain mail to keep your skin from getting scraped or pinched. Plus, I doubt armor absorbed sweat, and those suits were murder in hot weather. Recall Dr. Johnson and his non-mineral underwear policy.

We got *cotton* from Egypt—Arabic *ḳuṭn*. Marco Polo wrote about the cotton of *Mosul*, a city on the trade route (and the etymological root) for *muslin* (though there are those who have *muslin* originating further east, in *Masulipatnam*, India). Cotton grows from a seed *boll*, which, like *bowl*, is cognate to *ball*, as is the boll weevil that weaves through the boll.

Unsurprisingly, we get *canvas* from Latin *cannabis*—"hemp." But *canvas*'s offspring *canvass* has a winding and weird history. In the sixteenth century, it began as "shake or sift through loosely-woven hemp cloth." It evolved into "to sort" > "to discuss" > "to ask for support." *Burlap* is *burro*'s cousin; both are hairily rough.

For *khaki* twill, the British adopted Urdu *khak*, the color of dust. Imperial Britain also brought us "India rubber." *Rubber* reflects its first use: for "rubbing out." Throughout the British Empire, a *rubber* was an eraser. Definitely not in America.

We tap the South American Quechua language for the *kauchuk* tree, which provides the white liquid *Latex*. This brand name and the liquid resemble Latin *lac, lactis*: "milk." The *lactose* family descends from Greek *galaxias*, which gave us *galaxy*. One galaxy that looks like milk sprinkled across the night sky: the *Milky Way*. By the way, *lettuce* was named for the milky-looking fluid in its ribs. The word *milk* itself goes back to PIE *h₂melǵ*, which originally meant "rub" (like milking a cow).

Corduroy consists of parallel cords between which there are furrows called wide-wales or pin-wales, since a *wale* is a "vale" or valley. They say *duroy* was a rough fabric made in England in the 1700s. I believe them, since *durus* = "hard."

Meanwhile, a *corduroy road* protects the traveler from marshy terrain by means of logs placed side by side. Bumpy, but better than the bog.

When, unlike *Lycra*, fabric names *do* mean something, they're all over the place.

The French term *velours croché* ("hooked velvet") gave us *Velcro*.

Residents of the Channel island *Jersey* started knitting wool garments in the Middle Ages. (We inherit *knit* from *cnotta*, "knot" in Old English.) Wool abounded in the sheep-intensive British Isles, and knitting was easier than weaving, for which you needed daylight. Like the sun-averse cottages in hot countries, northern houses had negligible windowage, to resist not heat but cold and wind. Besides, a loom takes up a lot of space. Knitting is compact, and also portable. You can't take weaving equipment out for a coffee *klatch* (German "gossip") or down to the beach to welcome your menfolk home.

The source of *gossip*, by the way, is Old English "godsibb." A *sibb* was a kinsperson (not necessarily a sibling). A *godsibb*, godparent, came to mean any nosy, chatty (usually) female, much like a Yiddish *yenta*, and before you go feminist, remember this was the Middle Ages.

Woven cloths have little give, but stretchier knit material was good for fishermen's active-wear. Another plus: wool was somewhat waterproof due to the greasiness of *lanolin*—"wool oil."

You probably know that *-ol* = "oil": *Petrol*, oil from rock. *Menthol*, mint oil. *Linoleum*, heavy cloth stiffened with linseed oil. *Vaseline* was "vasoline," which combined German "water"—*Wasser*, *w* pronounced *v*—and *oleum*. Plain Latin *oleum* was olive oil, later incarnate in the person of *Olive Oyl*, Popeye's girlfriend. As incarnate as celluloid will permit.

À propos of petrol, at some point you'll be needing the noun *petrichor*: the smell of rain on dry (or stony) earth. *Ichor* is the blood of the gods.

A thirteenth-century German document avers that the Irish islands produced the *Aran Jumper* (UK *jumper* = US "sweater"). The garment was knit of thick yarn the color of a clean sheep. Like the jersey, it was optimal seagoing wear, although after a while lanolin's natural waterproofing throws in the towel. But don't worry; the Aran sweater can absorb a third of its weight in water and not feel wet to the touch. *Jumper* probably began, far from the chilly Irish seas, as Arabic *jubba* (like the Muslim *djibbah* kaftan). The Aran sweater's patterns, with their motifs convoluted like Celtic sculpture, were passed down through generations: a diamond stitch represents farmers' fields; a cable stitch, rope. A family's stitch-code helped identify a drowned fisherman.

No fewer than three British aristocrats are big names in knitwear.

First, consider Lord Cardigan, commander of the Battle of Balaclava in the Crimean War, who led his men to death in the *Charge of the Light Brigade.* (Tennyson provides stats:

> Half a league, half a league,
> Half a league onward,
> All in the valley of Death
>   Rode the six hundred
> . . .
> Cannon to right of them,
> Cannon to left of them,
> Cannon in front of them
>   Volleyed and thundered.)

Crimean-War fashion gave us the knit face-covering *balaclava* now worn by skiers in frigid weather and by felons seeking anonymity.

Lord Cardigan used to sport a button-up sweater-jacket known today as the *cardigan,* as modeled by Mr. Rogers. Cardigan reported to Lord Raglan. Later, after Raglan's arm was amputated at Waterloo, he favored jackets with the front sleeve seam running from neck to armpit. For example, the *Raglan sleeve* look appears in tee-shirts where shoulders and sleeves differ from the torso in color.

Lastly, we honor Lord Kitchener, the general and commander-in-chief in Khartoum who invented the *Kitchener stitch*, grafting two pieces of a military sock into a seam that wouldn't chafe soldiers' toes.

Let's touch on only a few of our myriad wool metaphors. To name three: *woolgathering* (daydreaming) has a literal source—wandering around collecting tufts of shorn fleece blown away by the wind (no need to be attentive). *Dyed in the wool*, meaning "through-and-through," describes an item whose wool was dyed before it was knit or woven, i.e., more thoroughly. A lying lawyer might *pull the wool over a judge's eyes*—yank his wig down across his face.

The word *wool* (*wull* in Old English) descends via German *Wolle* back to Latin *vellus*, "fleece." Charmingly, German "cotton" is *Baumwolle*, "tree-wool." Another *Baum* is *Tannenbaum*, fir tree, whence come both tannic acid and the surname *Tenenbaum*.

I'll end the fabric chapter with a nautical digression. *Baum* provides the noun *boom*—not the sound but the horizontal pole at the bottom of a sail. It was initially just a skinny tree-trunk: to *sail close to the wind* is to risk a sudden swing of the boom, walloping crew members in the temples. As a metaphor, the phrase ≈ "playing with fire."

Along with the boom, your sail needs a mast for vertical support. At sea and your mast breaks? Improvise a *jury rig*. Multiple choice question. The origin of an emergency *jury rig*? 1) *jour*, French "day"—a name for a solution that may last no more than a day. 2) From Latin *adjutare*—"help," like *adjuvant* therapy, such as surgery after chemo. 3) Short for "injury" to the mast.

Answer: No one knows. And here's another etymology no one knows: The phrase *jury-rig* may have blended with *jerry-built* to form *jerry-rigged*; all three words have a similar meaning. But *jerry-built* exists in its own right and means shoddily or hastily constructed. We have two rival etymologies for *jerry-built*. 1) It might allude to a one-time Liverpool construction company. 2) Personally, I prefer it as a reference to the walls of Jericho, which came tumbling down after Joshua's men orbited them daily for a week: his priests blasted the city with seven trumpets of rams' horns, whereupon Joshua's men shouted with a great shout, much as the wolf huffed and puffed and blew down the jerry-built houses of Pigs I and II. Anyway, as God had promised, they saw the walls "fall down flat."

10

Walk the Talk

Wandering

If your attention is wandering, take a break. Longfellow advised readers to *fold their tents, like the Arabs/And as silently steal away.* While you're gone, I myself will observe the Russian pre-voyage custom of sitting in silence for a few moments to collect one's thoughts.

Longfellow was referring to the Bedouins who break camp and mosey along to another dune or, if upwardly mobile, to a nice caravanserai with all the amenities. Myself, if I go nomad, I'd rather be a gypsy, which would also be a good bumper sticker. The *Roma*, footloose migrants who reached Europe from India via Romania, were thought to be *Egyptians*—hence "gypsies."

As wanderers, the Roma are outsiders by definition. They've always been maligned. They stole your horses. They begged. They *gypped* you. Less opprobrious, when you *crossed someone's palm with silver,* the typical someone was a mercenary gypsy fortuneteller. The Nazis called them racially inferior: murdered by the tens of thousands in the occupied regions and death camps, their numbers were drastically reduced; but three quarters of them are reckoned to have survived.

In the UK, especially Ireland, itinerants are called "Travellers." They mostly speak English, though some speak Irish

Traveller Cant, a mixture of English and *Shelta* (often claimed to be Irish Gaelic for "walkers").

Cant is related to the Latin verb *cantare* and *chanter*—again the French soften the hard *c* to a "*sh*" sound. A cant is a language used by a particular group, like the British *Rogues' Cant*, aka *Thieves' Cant* (also called *Peddler's French*). Even today British jailbirds use *Elizabethan Cant* when conducting private drug business.

From their work mending pots and pans, Travellers were also known as *tinkers* (tinsmiths)—as in John le Carré's *Tinker, Tailor, Soldier, Spy*. Speaking of spies, Travellers are not the same as *fellow-travelers*—Communist sympathizers who are not official "card-carrying members" of the Party.

Speaking of those idealized "classless societies," the Greek phrase *hoi polloi*, meaning "the masses," comes with the "the" (*hoi*) built in. A more common, less justifiable redundancy is the extra "is": "The reason *is is* he's a Libra."

Regarding people in motion and the proletariat: *mobile*.

When the populace go rebellious, they're a *mob*, which is short for *mobile vulgus*—the common people easily "moved" to riot. When Verdi says "*La donna è mobile*," he means women are fickle. Before quitting *mobile*, consider the *automobile*. *Auto* means not automatic but "self"—as in *autoimmune* (your immune system attacking yourself) or *autocracy*, rule by (one dictator's) self. In Britain your phone is a *mobile*, not a *cell*. *Mobile, Alabama*, however, is named after a Native American tribe.

But *vulgus* did not always suggest "rabble." The *Vulgate* was the fourth-century translation of the Bible from Greek into Latin, a language known only to educated men, a tiny percent of the population (for the one text they needed, the illiterate relied on the parish priest's spoken words). Ben Jonson (b. 1572) claimed Shakespeare knew "smalle Latine and lesse Greeke"— typical for one of common birth.

From *mobile* let's revisit the topic of transport, supplementing Chapter III: The Romans could hardly have predicted how far their preposition *trans* ("across") would carry the future world. Still, despite their incomplete mastery of satellite/broadcast communications, they'd understand the smashing together of *transmit* and *responder* into the portmanteau word *transponder*. No *tramcars* on the Appian Way, but in "tramcar" they might spy *trans* + *carrus* (cart) and would guess we were talking vehicular conveyance.

But faced with some other modern *trans* terms they'd go, *Huh? Transfer RNA? TransPlanckian?* What about *transgender people?* The closest the Greeks would come would be *hermaphrodite*, from the mixed-gender son of Hermes and Aphrodite. By the way, *trans* = "across" and *cis* = "on this side." A *cisgender* person sticks with his/her birth gender.

Train derives from Latin *trahere*, "drag"—not as in a transvestite's dress, but the verb: a train is a pulled thing. From railroads to a bride's *train* to the verb *to train* (potty-*train*ing), you're drawing something or someone forward.

As Good as Your Word

11

Speak of the Devil

I admit I've poked a little fun at Proto-Indo-European, but I'll just mention now that even *pre*-PIE, the word "evil" existed in the form of Hittite *huwapp*. Getting from *huwapp* to *evil* seems like a stretch until you look at intermediate forms *upelo* and *ubel*.

Another term for wickedness is *enormity*: originally "outside ethical norms." *Enormous* didn't focus on extreme size until the early nineteenth century.

You doubtless know *666* as "the Number of the Beast," alias the Antichrist, alias Satan. The Book of Revelations says Satan lived in Pergamum (in today's Turkey). Perhaps he summered there when Hell got too hot. The thing to know about the word *Pergamum*: it was the source of *parchment*.

The *pentagram*, a five-pointed symbol (*pente-* derives from the cute PIE *penkwe*), was copyrighted by a particular religious organization, the Church of Satan. Some schools once forbade students to wear it, but administrators were foiled (a literal case of *Curses, foiled again!*) by the students' rights to freedom of religion.

The Church of Satan does not worship Satan. It practices "greater and lesser magic" and occasionally uses a woman as an altar. Women are instructed to dress provocatively during rites. Rituals: Lust rituals (orgasm-producing), destruction rituals (to do harm), compassion rituals (weeping is a goal).

If you're ever feeling possessed, just say "*Vade retro satanas*": instant exorcism, available since the fifteenth century. Besides telling Satan to get out of your face, you can curse his followers with church *Comminations* (same root as "minatory" and "menace"). Sample: *Cursed is he that removeth his neighbor's landmark*—a sin right up there with adultery and slaughter. The word *neighbor* started out as "near-dwelling." Shifting a boundary-marker to enlarge your own field is malicious, but at least advantageous to you and thus understandable. Not sociopathic, like *he that maketh the blind [man] to go out of his way* (with intentionally wrong directions).

The Commination rite sends sinners into "fire and brimstone . . . where is weeping and gnashing of teeth." (For centuries the word *gnash* has been exclusively about teeth, the only direct object we ever hear.) If you're ever pew-side during this particular service, request a kinder and more lyrical fate for yourself: *Purge me with hyssop, and I shall be clean . . . wash me, and I shall be whiter than snow. Brimstone* is sulfur, "burnt stone"; as for *hyssop*, I can tell you that it's a "subshrub."

A witch's *hex*, meanwhile, has nothing to do with six or 666 and everything to do with its actual source "hag"—*hagzusa* in Old German.

To speak of the devil, the *devil's advocate* was the church lawyer appointed to argue against canonizing a sainthood-candidate. His due diligence usually involved debunking miracles. Good man to have on your forensics team, where *forensics* stems from *forum* (a public place or courtroom) and refers to both the art of formal debate and crime science.

Strong Language. In 2020 a mothers' group castigated a Burger King ad for the phrase: "Damn, that's good." When I was a child, the blasphemous *damn* was not used by the best people, at least not publicly (though the best people have always deemed it inoffensive when it means "condemn"). For swearing, if you needed an ejaculation (a word still used in the 1950s to mean "exclamation"), your workaround was *darn.* Or try either *dagnabbit* or *doggone it* as a droll Spooneristic play on "God damn it." Hint: used other than ironically, either of these words should alert you to flee the speaker *pronto.* Another folksy expletive, *Jiminy Cricket,* is a euphemism for Jesus Christ. A *euphemism* = speaking good of; a *blasphemy* = a bad saying.

12

Speak No Evil
Religion

Religion is weird (from Old English *Wyrd*, "fate"). And some of our vocabulary has surprising religious origins. Christianity, for one, left us a goodly legacy of words-gone-secular.

The British *bloody* is probably a slurred version of "by Our Lady," less offensive than it once was but still not what you expect to hear on your grandmother's lips, even if she's an atheist.

Cretin is a corruption of the Swiss French dialect word for "Christian." Thanks to mountainous terrain, Alpine villages were isolated and somewhat inbred; here, eighteenth-century children with congenital deficits were labeled *crestins*, because a cretin was a human being under God's special protection.

The word *silly* derives from German *Seele* (soul). En route to Britain, somewhere around the Netherlands, it became *sillich*, "soul-like." A simpleton was *silly*—all he had was a soul.

Regarding *sillich*, the suffix *lich* gave us our adverb-ending *-ly* as well as *-like*. By the way, if it were up to me, you couldn't use "like" as a conjunction. But I'm the only person in the English-speaking world who holds out for "as if" or "as though."

"Souls" became a generic term for "persons." If you learn that "the ship's manifest lists twenty-two souls aboard," you know how many people to check on when you answer their SOS ("Save our souls") or *Mayday!* (an anglicized form of French *m'aidez!*, "help me!").

Speaking of unhappy events, it wasn't only old-time pagans who practiced animal sacrifice. *Santería*, from Latin *sanctus* ("holy") is a Caribbean/African religion controversial in the US due to such rites. *Sacrifice* literally means "make sacred."

By the way and annoyingly, sacreligious has no etymological link to "religion," not to mention that it's not a word. The word is *sacrilegious*. *Sacri-lege* = "sacred" + "take away." The root of *religion* is "to bind," which is what *ligaments* (connective tissue) do.

There's a famous case of sacrilege, the sorry story of a man we met above when he was a 16-litre wine-bottle. To host a banquet, King Belshazzar, what a jerk, stole a few sacred goblets from the Temple.

Well, *you don't mess around with Jim*, namely God. During his drunken feast, Belshazzar saw the ghostly graffiti that was the original *writing on the wall*. You don't usually hear of *writing on the wall* heralding a happy future, and for Belshazzar it was bad news. The words were MENE MENE TEKEL UPHARSIN. The Akkadian language must be very compressed and efficient, because a lot of data was crammed into those words: Your kingdom is about to go belly up, like *now*. You've been weighed on the scales and found wanting. Your territory is being split between the Medes and the Persians.

Belshazzar's daughter Vashti, whose formidable lineage is described in the Midrash, was granddaughter of another wine bottle—Nebuchadnezzar, famous for Babylon's Hanging Gardens. She soon married the Persian king Ahasuerus (Xerxes), another party animal who, during another banquet, ordered her to dance (naked) for his guests.

His advisors attributed her refusal to nothing so tame as modesty. The obvious conclusion: she'd grown a tail she was embarrassed to reveal. Ahasuerus dumped her for Esther, who eventually saved the Jews from slaughter at the hands of Haman. Haman cast lots to determine a date for the assault; the day was named *Purim*—"lottery."

Aside: *Belshazzar* in Greek is *Balthazar*, the name of one of the Eastern Magi who (along with Caspar and Melchior) visited the Christ child. Speaking of the Wise Men, the gadget that contains (frank)incense is a *censer* (not a *censor* or *sensor*). Homonyms, never easy.

While we're warding off evil: Since the fourteenth century, the Pope has been guarded by his personal secret service, the Swiss Guards. They're hardly secret, though; they wear yellow-and-blue-striped clown suits. Each one is also equipped with a speared battle-axe and a Glock 19 to cover all contingencies. Being neutral, the Swiss have often hired themselves out as mercenaries to every Tom, Dick, Harry, and Pius. Since the fifteenth century, European royalty have employed units from the Swiss army as guards; the only Swiss Guards remaining are these mostly-ceremonial papal security officers.

Secular but equally fanciful (incidentally) is the get-up of the *Beefeaters* who defend the Tower of London in navy-blue or red trenchcoats with fussy gold trappings. Their name? One of their early perks was all-you-can-eat meals up at the palace, including meat, once a treat.

Religion, of course, does a brisk business in eternity. To access the afterlife, I recommend a *psychopomp* (*pompos* = Greek "conductor")—a guide to get your soul (*psyche*) to wherever it's headed, which might entail anything from slogging up the cumulus to fording the Stygian shoals. And you have options.

We've already heard a lot about Hermes. And his job description includes soul-conducting. Charon, oarsman of the Styx, heads up the river unit. *Styx* means "hateful," and who liked the entry to Hades?

Odin's girl-Valkyries, "choosers of the slain," will lead you to Valhalla if 1) you're Norse, 2) are slain in battle, and 3) Odin doesn't blackball you.

The Qur'an designates Izraeel as the Angel of Death, who removes the soul from the body and stows it in Barzakh pending Judgment Day. Apparently the soul of an evil individual can adhere stubbornly to the body, requiring multiple angels to pound the face and back of the decedent. I suppose that shakes it loose.

In ancient Egypt, a praying mantis, the "bird-fly," piloted souls to the underworld.

The Christian chaperone for the soul is Saint Michael. As an *archangel* ("chief angel"), Michael is God's direct report on the celestial org chart. Besides steering your soul to the hereafter, he's V.P. of War—"defender of Israel." It was Michael who led an angel squad in an attack on Satan, whose remit is testing the virtue of mortals.

Michael, whose name means a question: "Who could be like God?" kept *Abraham*, "Father of Nations," from sacrificing Isaac. He also saved *Lot* ("veil"—his covered eyes did not look back) when *Sodom* (the sinful city that gave us the word *sodomy*) and Gomorrah were wrecked. Too bad Lot's wife pulled an Orpheus on the non-retrospection clause. She was not so lucky, being turned into a pillar of salt. I wonder why she's always known as "Lot's Wife" when she has a perfectly good name, namely *Edith* (Hebrew "Ado").

Speaking of the pillar of salt, some Spanish girls are baptized with the (non-saline) religious name *Pilar*, honoring the image of Mary seen on a pillar in Saragossa. You often find Mary somewhere behind a Spanish female name: *Maria de Lourdes* commemorates another shrine. *Dolores* = "Mary of the Sorrows." *Mercedes* = "Mercy," one of Mary's trademark virtues. The names *Asunción* and *Concepción* refer to highlights in the Virgin's life. *Rosario*, which sounds like a masculine name, stands for *Maria del Rosario* ("rosary").

"Christian names" is a former term for first names; in Catholic countries you were as good as required to name your baby after a saint. Two parentheses regarding saints:

1) Maybe, like me, you've logged a fair amount of time asking yourself, what the heck is a *Latter-Day Saint*? Answer:

the earliest Christians called themselves "saints"; latter-
day refers to "restorationism"—to the original apostolic
church. When Joseph Smith revealed the Book of Mormon, he explained that *Mormon* = more + *mon* ("good" in
Egyptian).

2) To canonize, specifically (see above) to certify for saint-
hood, in general means to "make official," from Greek
kanon, "rule."

Sub-parenthesis on a sound-alike:

Latin *canna*, hollow "reed" or "cane," gives us a) with -*ul*,
the surgical cannula, b) *canyon*, from *cañon*, a "hollowed out
place," and c) *canon*'s homonym: the artillery *cannon*. A *cannon*,
from *canone*, is nothing more than a huge-caliber reed. A *cali-
ber* is a "measure," as in "calibrate"; its distant ancestor is Greek
kalapous, "shoemaker's last."

Sub-sub-parenthesis: Greek *pous* = "foot." Append *pous* to
the beginning of *(o)edema* ("swelling") and you get *Oedipus*. His
foot was swollen from being chained to a stake in the boondocks. This was an attempt to foil fate, and we know how well
that works. Incidentally, we get *boondocks* from the American
occupation of the Philippines, where in the Tagalog language
bundok = "mountain."

The chapter on religion now ended, a spiritual "good-
bye," i.e., "God be with you," which got blurred into *good-bye*.
Likewise, *adios*, *adieu*, and *addio* say "go with God." But most
languages include a secular option. *Hasta la vista, au revoir, arri-
vederci*, and *auf Wiedersehen*, Swedish *vi ses*—"until we see each
other again."

13

Baby Talk
Children

We inherit "child" from Anglo-Saxon *cildhama*, "womb-home."

Strictly Speaking. Besides disease, today's parents fear the psychologically troubling; modern culture is as full of menace as the deceptively-dubbed "action movie," where "action" means carnage. Although this stuff probably won't turn a kid into a brute, it may up his tolerance to violence.

Incidentally, a category new to the American Motion Picture movie ratings: besides the usual suspects (*nudity, language, violence,* and let's not forget *smoking*), watch out for *meteorological brutality.*

Worry about *kidnapping* (originally "kid-nabbing") is perennial; in the last half-century our dread of pedophiles—"child-lovers"—has increased with awareness. Often we look back longingly to a nobler era, saying with Cicero, *O tempora o mores!* ("Oh, our times, oh, our culture!") Not so in the case of Greek "pederasty" (*pede*, "child" + *eros*, "erotic love"): institutionalized pedophilia, men using teenage boys for sex (TMI alert: not oral or anal but between the thighs). Europeans later called homosexuality "Greek love."

An interruption: The acute reader will question the root *ped-*. Surely it means "foot"?, you interject; what about *pedestal* and *pedestrian*? Answer: One form of *pous*, the Greek for "foot," is *podi*, as in *pseudopod*, a "phony foot" that oozes from an amoeba, a creature that evolved long before the sophisticated *arthropods* with "jointed feet." *Arthritis* = pain in the joints, which might take you to a *podiatrist*.

A sub-interruption: In poetry, a *foot* is a repeated metrical unit. In ancient Greek, when all poetry was recited orally, you tapped your foot to the rhythm.

Maybe not coincidentally, the first Greek cities to adopt pederasty were those where athletes exercised in the nude: the root of *gymnasium* is *gymno* ("naked"). The *gymnasium*, however, evolved into a college that taught both athletics and academics. In Western and Central Europe today, a *gymnasium* is a secondary school with an intellectual focus.

Anxiety about children's safety is welcome and overdue—up to a point.

Worried about older kids, some colleges provide *trigger warnings* on any course content that could trigger Post-Traumatic Stress. (*Trigger* has come a long way—it's an offshoot of *Trek*, Dutch "to pull," as an ox-cart.) Talking of trauma and triggers, I'd say the course syllabus pales beside the movie violence many students have cut their teeth on.

Here's an actual case (though half of you readers won't agree) of *o tempora o mores* nostalgia: In the 1970s, I heard a learning specialist sneer at the old days "when we thought the role of education was to fill children with knowledge. Now we know better. It's our job to provide not facts but learning skills for the child's *toolbox*," a metaphor that should be murdered. I say you can't operate on thin air. Tools are useless without lumber, where lumber is the actual material the tools turn into something beneficial.

Kindergartens, paradoxically, often do teach real content—numbers, letters, natural science. *Kindergarten* = German "children's garden."

Parents ban some fairy tales as too scary, but the whole point of the stories is the thrill of the *recognizably unreal* (real derives from Latin *res*, "thing"). Beanstalks infested with felonious giants. Troll-patrolled bridges. Tom Thumb, homunculus, floundering in a bowl of soup; his thumb-sized girl counterpart abducted by a toad ("thumb" and "tumor" share a common—distant—origin). Maybe we get a *frisson* from Bluebeard's meat-hooked ex-wives, but do children really believe in a wardrobe full of spouses?

Along these lines, please pardon a parenthetical paragraph on children's stories: First, there's the forgotten and graphic picture-book *Struwwelpeter* ("straw-headed Peter"), whose great sin is failure to comb his hair. The book's grisly punishments resemble a collection of ghastly tetrameters starring Little Willie (the name *William* = "determination-helmet"). One of his ghoulish penalties:

Little Willie took a mirror,
Licked the mercury right off,
Thinking in his childish folly,
It would cure the whooping cough.

Little Willie now is standing
On the golden shore,
For what he thought was H_2O
Was H_2SO_4.

An aside on Willie's *mirror*: it descends from Latin *admirari* ("to regard or admire"), as in "miracle" or *Miranda*—"one to be admired." Speaking of which, your *Miranda rights* are based on the 1963 case of Ernesto Miranda, who was arrested and not briefed on his legal rights.

Let's leave the children chapter with a different take on youngsters, namely *pedophobia*, "extreme fear of babies and children." A special case of this disorder is *ephebiphobia*, "fear of teenagers," which seems eminently sane.

Don't confuse pedophobia with *pediophobia*: for its victims, according to *Healthline*, "seeing or thinking about dolls can cause anxiety that is so intense they may become frozen with fear." Dolls, always a threat. But if the disorder "negatively affects your day-to-day functioning," seek a professional for "exposure therapy or systematic desensitization." The gold-standard pediophobia treatment facility is the History Center of Olmsted County (Rochester, Minnesota), home to the Creepy Doll Collection.

14

What's the Magic Word?

Fortune-telling

Talk Is Cheap. A previous chapter began with gypsies, often associated with fortune-telling. Here we begin with a few other options in this fertile field.

Divination can have very specific goals. Consider *dowsing*. A *dowser* (origin unknown), or *water-witch*, strolls around with a forked "divining rod" to discover underground resources (oil or treasure, but usually water).

Well, there's a sucker born every minute. Call them charlatans, but feel free to take out a subscription to *Dowsing Today: The Journal of the British Society of Dowsers*, where a catalog includes copper and steel dowsing rods of all lengths, not to mention the Original Cameron Aurameter, a "versatile tool with the action of a bobber." Seriously and snark aside, however, these dowsers follow a Code of Ethics covering decent behavior not necessarily evident in other professions. The one important thing about dowsing is not to confuse it with another water-word: *dousing*, which means "drenching." Another homonym pair and speller's nightmare: *auger* (a hole-boring tool) and *augur*.

An *augur*, which derives from Latin *avis* (bird) + *garrire* (to talk), was a Roman priest-cum-prophet. Don't confuse him with an auspex, from *avis* + *specere* ("to look at"), who specialized in auspicious interpretations of bird-flight. For a time these *aus-*

pices monopolized the clairvoyant market. As years passed, however, the *haruspex*, "reader of animal entrails," began to muscle in on the bird business. (*Haru-*, from *ghere-* ("guts"), takes us back again to PIE territory.)

Recall, by the way, that *gelomancy* is divination by laughter. Graduates of Laughter Online Institute might go this route.

But there are many, many forecasting technologies available today.

True, some systems involve much advanced technology, e.g., time travel. Not that classical antiquity lacked cutting-edge science. Two examples:

1) The Sibyl, vaunted psychic, conveniently headquartered in Cumae not far from Naples, would write your fate on oak leaves. Then, after the wind disarranged them, you had to put them together like a moving-target jigsaw puzzle. With luck, you'd manage to extrapolate a cryptic message.

2) At Delphi in Greece, another prophetess (who channeled Apollo) sat on a tripod and went into trances where she spewed out gobbledygook, which was taken as oracular. A priest or priestess translated, most likely saying whatever they felt like.

   One school claims that ethylene gases from volcanic fissures triggered her state of ecstasy (*ecstasy* means "standing outside one's self"). Others go with epileptic-like seizures caused by chewing the leaves or inhaling the smoke of the oleander shrub, aka dogbane, active ingredient digitoxigenin: the *oleander* is named for its passing resemblance to the olive, *olea*.

Like the ancient priestesses' blather, onomatapoetic *ololygmancy* prognosticates with sound—namely the howlings of dogs. In times when the world was rural and people had constant contact with animals, it's no wonder that, leaving aside the small detail of interpretation, beasts had prophetic power.

If you have access to a boiled donkey's head, you can see your future via *cephalonomancy* without leaving home. Other animal parts you can augur with include: the cracks on a turtle's shell, *plastromancy*. Beetle tracks, s*katharomancy*. Feces, *spatilomancy*, of which a sub-specialty is *stercomancy*, reading seeds in bird excrement (remember Sterculius and the chocolate tree). Let's not omit *myomancy*, rodent behavior. More convenient for us today is *apantomancy*, divination by chance meetings with animals.

Or, forget animals; humans are handier.

Try *urticaraomancy* to decrypt itches. *Dririmancy* uses blood drips: Dexter's is an ancient art. There's always *styramancy*—patterns in chewed gum (*styrax* is natural balsam-resin). From the same root is *styrofoam*, "a synthetic aromatic hydrocarbon polymer made from the monomer styrene." Its claim to fame is that it doesn't decompose until the Apocalypse, if then.

The bad news is that a wad of Wrigley's or Bazooka—or any of these -mancies—isn't worth a rat's bezoo to an amateur; you need a professional interpreter, which sounds like a job with easy money and bears looking into.

At any rate (preferably a high one) at least consider setting up shop as a (faux) psychic. The soothsaying business (*sooth* = "truth") involves no overhead, no license or certification, no training at all! Start with simple *retromancy*—predicting the future by looking over your shoulder. Myself, if I ever go pro, I'll be practicing *margaritomancy* as mentioned earlier, although I've toyed with reading the future in typos, and depending on your keyboard skills, you too can try it.

15

The Last Word

Death

A child barely gives a passing thought to death: he'll be infinity years old when it happens. An adult, however, occasionally experiences a *memento mori*—which literally says "Remember to die" (exactly the kind of thing that might slip your mind, so add it to your to-do list, and don't spell it "momento").

This little chapter is light on etymology, heavy on irreverence. *Chapter*, by the way, like *chef* above, goes back to Latin *caput, capitis*, "head." Other derivatives include *cap*; the music-score directive *da capo*, "from the top"; capital punishment (beheading); and the orthographically pesky *capital/Capitol*.

Sad to say, a political or cultural rock star will often die an inglorious death. Attila the Hun died of a nosebleed in 453. Tamerlane, the Mongol conqueror, who vied with Attila for copyright on the title "Scourge of God," succumbed to a head cold. One story claims Elvis perished from drug-induced constipation, not that I ought to contribute to that rumor. Sennacherib the Assyrian was squashed beneath a massive statue of a bull.

We'll discuss animals in the next two chapters, but what about a pet's demise?

Millions of us face another type of brush with death. The rainbow is the symbol of two international organizations. It's widely celebrated as the emblem of the LGBTQ movement. But you may not know of the Rainbow Bridge Support Community for mourners of pets: "Whether furry, feathered or scaled, all are welcome here."

A Rainbow Residency Memorial Membership buys a virtual cemetery plot where you can leave new toys and flowers as well as add more memories and photos, change the music, and more. "At the Candle Ceremony—9 p.m. weekly EST, other times internationally—we honor our furchildren and feathered friends." The grief support community donates to animal shelters partial proceeds of their sales of products like the Forever Spot Pet Shroud and personalized Mourninglights Candles.

But: to repudiate my snarky tone, I too have mourned for pets, and the grief is real.

Turning to a Christian view of animal death, Pope Francis, namesake of St. Francis of Assisi, patron of animals, believes in an animal afterlife. Coincidentally (speaking of popes and the Rainbow Bridge), the source of *pontiff* is *pontifex*, "bridge-builder." The Gospel says not a single sparrow shall fall on the ground unless God wills it. (Incidentally, *Gospel* came from German *gut-spiel*, which became English "good story." Although *Spiel* = German for "game," the Yiddish *spiel*—long recitation—may derive from High German *spellon*, "to tell." *Spiel* is cousin to *spell*, "fable.") Speaking of papacy and birds, a turkey's *pope's nose* is its rump, more formally, its *pygostyle*. *Steatopygia* means fat buttocks, if you've been looking for the scientific name.

A *potter's field* is a paupers' burial place: clay soil, though excellent for pottery, was no good for crops, so it was put to use for graves. The phrase is a gift of Judas Iscariot, the hit man paid thirty pieces of silver for betraying Christ. He remorsefully gave back the blood money, which was used to buy a potter's field for Jesus's burial.

Since the seventeenth century, it was a *funeral-undertaker* who managed the burial; somehow the all-purpose term *undertaker* (i.e., one who undertakes something) grew specific. And don't forget the old saw, "It's not the cough that carries you off; it's the coffin they carry you off in."

Some say "internment" instead of *interment* in hopes that the grave is a temporary spot.

As matter of taste and fact, I don't care for the genteel euphemism *to pass on*, and I care even less for *to pass*. Just personal opinion. On the irreverent side, to *kick the bucket* may have originated from kicking away your footrest when hanging yourself. More macabre is to take a *dirt nap*.

Talk the Hind Leg
Off a Donkey

16

Cat Got Your Tongue?

We love our pets, except in figures of speech—which are particularly unkind to cats. (When chatting with a Rainbow Bridger, do not mention that a lottery win has as much chance as *a wax cat in hell*.) We also drop the little feline *on a hot tin roof*. A *cat's paw* is the poor sucker who does the dirty work. We have *more than one way to skin a cat*. No wonder they're *scaredy-* and *fraidy-*.

They also seem to be obnoxious. What happens *when the cat's away*? Footloose and fancy-free, it goes on vacation and turns the house over to partying rodents. Cats *pussyfoot* around. They *eat the canary*. They *get your tongue*. They're secrets that get let *out of the bag*. Under the alias *Tom*, they lech along alleys. Their curiosity kills them. They're catty.

Cats have a high spook factor. They play mind-games—disembodied grins in Cheshire trees and quantum paradoxes in boxes, courtesy of Schrödinger.

But cats do know how to dress. The *cat's pajamas* (from Persian *pay-jama*, "leg-clothes") are something really dandy. And when it comes to kittens, it's all good. Going after the youth market, the Japanese *Hello Kitty* makes a fortune. In the 1950s, *kitten heels* for adolescent girls provided a step toward the high heels too adult for young teens. Then there's the seductress, the oxymoronic *sex kitten*—a *dis*ingenuous ingenue.

That's enough of cat concatenation.

Tongues Wag

Canines

Let's *go to the dogs*—man's best friends, although:

Canine is cognate to the word *cynic*, from the Latin *cynicus*, taken from the Greek word *kunikos*, colloquially used for "dog-like" and "ill-tempered." For us, of course, the cynic believes the worst of other's motives. Ancient Greeks used the label for a philosopher who believed in freedom from *typhus*—"smoke," as you recall. By typhus, the Cynics meant the fog of unenlightened ignorance. In fact, Cynicism endorsed natural virtue and a simple life.

Your canines are your *eye teeth*, the ones directly under your eyes; if you'd give your eye teeth for something, you want it enough to sacrifice something indispensable. Fashion footnote: the fabric pattern *houndstooth* is a checkered fabric of interlocked black-and-white, said to resemble canine teeth.

Dogs dog you. They hound you (from German *hund*). American colonists used to *put on the dog* when, lacking better leather, they made gloves and shoes from dog-skin to impress the neighborhood. A *hair of the dog* (that bit you) is a cur-cure for a hangover (note in passing that a French hangover is a "wooden throat"). And consider the fair-skinned British officer sent out to imperial India. What does the dunce do? *Mad dogs and Englishmen go out in the noonday sun.*

Speaking of mad dogs, Latin *rabies* = "rage." And speaking of hot weather, the miserable summer *dog days* are the period when Sirius, the Dog Star, is visible. At the opposite end of the thermostat, a *three-dog-night* in the Arctic is the point where the cold requires you to sleep with three dogs. And that's Arctic, not "Artic"; it's named for the Bear constellation. Greek *arktos* = "bear."

In fact, let's leave dogs for a moment and spend a couple of paragraphs on the bear. The name Bernard stems from *Bernhard*, "as hardy as a bear." But—except in Wall Street and the cottage where the self-involved trespasser Goldilocks makes herself at home—the bear gets low PR ratings. In France, a crude boor is called an *ours mal léché*, a "badly-licked bear." The licking motif may date back to ancient Rome: Right up through the Middle Ages, many believed a bear cub was born as a shapeless blob and had to be licked by its mother into the form of a bear.

Also in the ursine department, by the way: Instead of counting their chickens before they're hatched, the Danes, Dutch, and Polish "sell the fur before the bear is shot." In Germany, the raccoon is a "washing bear" (*Waschbär*); also in Sweden (*tvättbjorn*). The word "raccoon" comes to us from Algonquian *arahkunem*, "he scratches with his hands."

Credit Theodore Roosevelt for the *teddy bear*. In 1902 his fellow-hunters clubbed a bear. Roosevelt, when offered the honor of shooting it (as a notch on his belt), refused, but to put it out of its misery he had it killed. Unrelated is the *teddy* undergarment, a sexy camisole, underpants optional. A *Teddy-boy* (from "Edwardian") wore neo-foppish suits and a proto-Greaser hairdo; in the 1940s, Americans sported the even more farcical *zoot suit*, by which I mean you have to see it to believe it (*zoot* from "suit")—baggy in the leg, tight at the ankle.

That concludes the bears digression, by which I mean a considerable excursion. We return to dogs, mainly French ones.

The poodle is the German *Pudelhund*—"puddle-hound," a water dog (unlike the *chien terrier*, which goes after its prey by burrowing in the earth). The French poodle is the national dog of France, but would the French choose a Teutonic term? Never. The Gallic poodle is a *caniche*—bred to hunt ducks (*canards*). Actually, in a perennial second Franco-Prussian war, the French claim the original poodle forebear was their own *barbet*, described in the breed's website as rustic, rectangular, and rare—ranking 195th in AKC breed popularity. His whiskery jaws give him his name.

The French have a curious convention for naming purebred dogs. To register a dog in the official *Livre des origines françaises*, you must follow the letter-of-the-year protocol. If your dog is whelped in a *B* year, for example, its name has to begin with a *B*; 2020 was an *R* year.

The most enchanting dog idiom is "poodle-faking." A *poodle-faker* is a ladies' man who likes to spend time with women rather than messing around in manly sports or pursuits. He's not necessarily a flirt; he's not gay. More like a lapdog.

Some dog breeds take their names from places, e.g., the Spanish-bred *spaniel*. German speakers have been very active in developing canine varieties. The *Rottweiler Metzgerhund*, "butcher dog," once carted slaughtered meat to market in Rottweil. Many names reflect a breed's line of work (especially hunting lingo). *Schnauzer* = "snouter" (hence your Yiddish *schnoz*); *dachshund*, "badger dog" (see above). A *Shih tzu* is a "lion dog," from Chinese *shi*, "lion" and *gou*, "dog"—presumably named for its lion-like mane, not its lion-hunting prowess. *Chow chow* was a seventeenth-century term for all things Chinese.

Other species in genus *Canis* fare poorly, reputation-wise.

Take the jackal, a lazy scavenger too feckless to do his own killing—the janitor of animals who does the cleaning up. By extension a *jackal* is someone who does menial and degrading work for a boss (often as an accomplice in crime). You never hear of a noble jackal. Etymologically, he began in Sanskrit as a *srgala*.

Your coyote is vilified as a suburban *assassin*—the word is from the Arabic "*hashish*-eaters" who used the drug to psych themselves up for murder. Coyotes broadcast an unearthly yipping-baying; the panicky public thinks their nocturnal hootenannies are war dances prepping them for a toddler supper. Personally, I admire an animal who can throw his own solo voice to simulate the howling of a whole band (a *band*, incidentally, is not only a musical ensemble but also the official collective noun for coyotes, like a shoal of fish or a murder of crows).

And the wolf? The werewolf showcases its Protean nature. Like the ever-changing sea-god Proteus, a *protean* actor can play a wide range of roles. Bruce Willis is not a good example. The wolf is an adept shapeshifter who 1) disguises himself in sheep's clothing, 2) impersonates Red Riding Hood's grandma, and 3) can do a round-trip man > wolf > man in his capacity as a *werewolf*, where *were* (cognate to Latin *vir*) means "man."

We see *were* in the term *weregild* (*gild* as in "gilt" or "gold"); to the Anglo-Saxons *weregild* represented the value of a man's life—which depended on his social rank. *Weregild* = "man-money," the sum you owe his family in compensation if you kill him in an eleventh-century drunken mead-hall fracas, and you better pay it, too, or expect an eye-for-an-eye reply.

Here, incidentally, is a more recent case of graduated fee-for-slaughter: if you kill a prohibited game animal with a slingshot, the Wisconsin Department of Natural Resources fines you for the animal's value, which can range from $8.75 (a squirrel) to $2000 (an elk).

Returning to gold, German *Geld* gives us *gelt*, the money or gold-foil coins children get at Hannukah. The *guilder* was the pre-Euro Dutch currency. *Geld* shares a common ancestor with *yield*, as in "to pay or be worth." And don't *gild the lily*—embellish something that's already beautiful.

As a metaphor for hunger and poverty, the wolf's at your door—if not actually huffing and puffing. A certain trio of pigs performed a controlled experiment in home security, success rate only 33.3%.

Three pig parentheticals: 1) *Porpoise* comes from "pork-fish"; its nose resembled a pig's snout. 2) French pigs say not *oink* but *groin*, pronounce *groo-ă*, which in turn is a far cry from the Swedish swine's *nöff.* (While we're on noses, the Hideous Animal Prize goes to the proboscis monkey, honorable mention to the starnosed mole, except on second thought the mole wins by a nose. Gird your loins and Google a picture.)

In the story *Peter and the Wolf,* the wolf swallows live ducks whole. Tricky, since in this tale of musical instruments he's a French horn, which Prokofiev uses for the wolf's *leitmotif,* or "leading" musical theme. Prudently, Peter didn't behave like the waggish boy who cried "Wolf!" one time too many.

One nobler lupine creature was the she-wolf who suckled the twins Romulus ("little Rome") and Remus. After the latter's murder, Romulus went on to found Rome.

A wolf howls, preferably around a dacha containing Julie Christie and Omar Sharif in romantic extremis. Like the pigs' assailant, he's big and he's bad (the wolf, not Omar Sharif; Dr. Zhivago was a gentle part-time poet).

Our final canid: If you go back far enough, you find that German *Fuchs* (fox), was originally the word for "tail." Hunters claim this lush object as a trophy. Ridiculous comment: we all know the alpha in a pack is unique; he's *the* top dog. But as a perfect foxymoron, a policeman once warned me away from a den of alpha foxes.

18

The Horse's Mouth

The horse, a "solidungulate perissodactyl mammal," is so basic an animal in human history that it merits its own chapter, which includes one or two tall tales. To quote one radio pundit: "[It] was discovered due to a *tall-tale* sign that hinted it was there." Not impossible, I guess, but kind of a logical fallacy.

Farming. Fighting. Riding. Racing, too, where a *furlong*, which, while it sounds like an Old English Sheepdog, is actually an Old English combo of "furrow" and "long." (Hold that thought while I mention the unrelated *furlough*, from Dutch *verlof*—"for leave.") A furlong was the "length of a field," which made it pretty inexact until they standardized the word to mean about an eighth of a mile. English-speaking countries still measure race-course distances in furlongs. A *course* derives from Latin *cursus*, "running"—like *cursor*, *current*, and *cursory*.

Your plow animals, like the *QE2*, did not turn on a dime, so you used to plow in very long furrows to minimize the effort of turning your team (often not horses but bulky non-lithe oxen). In a culture where agriculture was always in your face, lines on a page looked like a plowed field, and the ox-maneuver also affected poetry: Latin *versus*, a "turn," gave its name to *verse*. Greek did the same; Greek for "turn" is *strophe*, which is also a poetic stanza. In fact, when chatting about ancient texts, you'll want the Greek term *boustrophedon—bous* ("ox") + *strophe*. *Boustrophedon* is an earlier script where alternate lines were read in alternate directions.

British postmen use the word to describe postal routes that go up one side of the street and then down the other. And who knows, some day you yourself may need the longer term *boustrophedon transform*, a mathematical thing involving $bk|k > 0$, enough said.

That team of oxen could plow about an *acre* (from Latin *ager*, "field") a day. A man moves faster, walking one *league*—three miles—per hour. This sounds like the beginning of a poxy word problem in arithmetic, so let's join that hiker in a *pint*, which is the mark that's "painted" (Latin *picta*) on a container measuring beer. *Pint*'s close cousins include such painted items as the *pinto* bean, the *pinto* horse, and Columbus's fastest ship, the *Pinta*; the Ford *Pinto* was engineered to burst into fatal flames.

Speaking of fire, ranchers used hot *brands* (burning embers, remember) to brand cattle—i.e., "label," as in commercial *brands*. *Brand-new* means "still hot from the forge. An aside on "rebranding": New York's *Roosevelt Hospital* changed its name to *Sinai West* as "one step in the rebranding process" for "consistent naming across the health system." More often institutions rename themselves after a big donor. *Avery Fisher Hall* in Lincoln Center has become *David Geffen Hall*, at the insistence of Geffen, who donated one hundred million dollars. A gift of $350 million was contingent on a name change to *Harvard T.H. Chan School of Public Health*.

But we've gotten far afield. The topic was horses.

Would you buy a used car without getting its stats? Just as a crooked car dealer can take miles off an odometer; a horse dealer can *lie through his teeth* and take years off the age of a horse that's *long in the tooth*. Readers with receding gums understand this phrase. Anyway, assess the horse's age by inspecting its mouth. Hence the etiquette tip concerning a freebie: *Don't look a gift horse in the mouth.*

By the way, pity the tooth, chronically badmouthed. Shakespeare's King Lear labels the ingratitude of his daughter Goneril (there's an unfortunate name) *sharper than a serpent's tooth.* The Old Testament is big on retaliation: *an eye for an eye, a tooth for a tooth.* Job, famous for his misfortune does escape *"by the skin of my teeth"*—an idiom from a Hebrew phrase meaning his teeth have fallen out and only his gums cling to his jawbones.

On make-believe equines:

According to toy-makers, 2015 was "the year of the unicorn." Hasbro sells this legendary beast as a "FurReal Friend." Aware, of course, that only a virgin can capture a unicorn, they named the toy "StarLily," where the lily symbolizes purity. Plus, unlike the Rainbow Bridge's fur baby, the FurReal Friend is immortal, and at $150 she should be. In Silicon Valley, on the other hand, a *unicorn* refers to the rare-as-a-unicorn start-up company that's worth a billion dollars or more.

Staying in the fable-zone, we come to the *gyascutus.* The *gyascutus* is a fabulous creature who has adapted to walking on hillsides by developing longer legs on the downhill side. A perfect marvel of evolution.

Better known than the gyascutus is the *centaur,* another freak of nature, a man grafted at the waistline onto a horse. It's said that the Aztecs, never having seen a man on horseback, thought the Conquistadors were terrifying, galloping, quadruped men.

The horse is all over the Greek myths.

Talking to a Brick Wall. The Trojan priest Laocoön warned the residents against taking in (being taken in by) the Trojan Horse. Beware of Greeks even when bearing gifts, he said. If there was any gift horse to look in the mouth, this was it. This story (according to me) springs from a germ of truth, by which I do not mean thirty men in a wooden animal's abdomen. In actuality, this piece of matériel obviously existed as a siege machine known as a "horse." Mind you, I prefer a ridiculous outsize soldier-stuffed hobby-horse deployed as distraction-artillery.

Like this creature allegedly admitted into the bosom of Troy, today's *Trojan horse* is a software virus that poses as a tempting app for you to blithely download.

Hippolyta, Queen of the Amazons, derives from two Greek roots: *hippo*, "horse," and *lysis*, which, you recall, means "unbind." (A store near me is spelled "Hyppolita," which is why you need etymology, although I confess to occasional trouble with *sybil* vs. *sibyl*.) According to Greek lore, these warlike equestriennes were called Amazons because they removed one breast (*a-mazos*—"without a breast") for greater proficiency in archery. They needed the remaining breast to steady the bow—maybe also to suckle babies, except 1) they weren't very into maternal matters, and anyway 2) they used mares as wet nurses.

The only paraphernalia they cared about was bows, arrows, horses, and chariots. But "paraphernalia" is *not* the *mot juste* here: it designates a *married woman's property*, and the Amazons were not into marriage either, or even men. So how the babies, you ask. The Amazons had sex with their male slaves just often enough to perpetuate the tribe.

Again, a legend is often based on a granule of fact; these ladies were most likely an actual man-hating tribe in Scythia or in what is now Turkey. But what about the Amazon River? It's nowhere near Greece. The river was named the *Rio Santa Maria de la Mar Dolce* until the Spanish ran into a pack of warlike tribeswomen in the area.

By the way, *Amazon.com* owes its name to an auditory error. It was originally called *Cadabra*, short (surely) for *abracadabra*—until, in another *b/v* metamorphosis, someone misunderstood *cadabra* as *cadaver*. No good, said Bezos. He chose *Amazon* to reflect the hugest river in the world. The Amazon horsewomen left a long legacy.

Google, too, based its name on size. Its founders, setting their sights on a mammoth search engine, called it Google for *googolplex*, a term invented by a mathematician's eight-year-old nephew who described it as all the zeroes you can write without getting bored. The boy made up *googol* as a ridiculous name for a ridiculous number. Googol is 10100, also known as 10googol or *10 duotregintillion*.

Anyway, so scary was Hippolyta that one of Hercules' twelve Labors was to steal her girdle. This was not your grandmother's *Playtex Living Girdle*, solid rubber that "lives and breathes with you." Rubber, *breathe?* Today's solution: *Spanx*—"compression" underwear made of *Spandex. Spandex* itself is a play on "expand." The brand *Spanx,* homonym of "spanks," is inspiredly buttocky and just a thought naughty.

Playtex was a portmanteau word—"play" grafted onto "latex." Nice threefer: *tex* also suggests "textile." "Play" positions their girdle as sportswear. Odd, since it was basically a non-stretchy (I'm guessing an elastic property around psi 1 lbF/in^2) miniskirt with steel garters appended mid-thigh to hold up your inelastic stockings (bend your knee in these stockings and you split their nylon kneecap into a *run,* a snag that unzips the nylon mesh into a narrow "ladder," the British term).

Whoa! I've strayed from horses.

Mum's the Word. The Amazon Hippolyta was the mother of Hippolytus, who was later seduced by his stepmother Phaedra. This ended badly. Cursed by his father, Theseus, Hippolytus galloped away, but despite his inherited equestrian skill, his horses—startled by a *hippokampos,* sea-monster—fatally dragged him into the crashing waves. Romans called the seahorse *hippocampus* (still its Linnaean name). Later its shape gave its name to a region in the brain.

Suggestion: For a boy's name with less baggage than *Hippolytus,* you could choose *Philip,* as in *phil,* "love," and *[h]ipp.*

On the large end, a *hippopotamus* is "a water horse": recall *potamos* = "river." *Mesopotamia* was the land between the Tigris and Euphrates rivers, also known as the battlefield of the Iraq war.

Incidentally, a river *delta* is shaped like the Greek letter Δ, *delta.* The Greeks got it from the Phoenician *daleth,* a "tent-door." I wish I had the time and space, and you the desire, to explore the Greek alphabetcetera.

Another *hippo* myth features *Hippodamia* ("she who masters horses"), who *played the field*—i.e., dated a lot of men. Her father to her suitors: "Here's the deal. Your horses race mine. Yours win, you get Hippodamia. Mine win, you die." Speaking of fields, this wasn't exactly a level playing field; his horses were given to him by Ares. Hippodamia or her boyfriend Pelops bribed her father's chariot-driver to fix the race, which he did by substituting beeswax for the metal in his axles. Note that the coupled sweetened the bribe by throwing in a night with Hippodamia.

Here we move to a recurring and disturbing motif in her husband's family, namely cannibalism. As a child, Pelops had been finely diced by his father Tantalus and served to the gods. Nasty. Luckily, the gods caught on quickly. Only one goddess tasted only one shoulder. When the boy was rebuilt, the gods' blacksmith Hephaestus forged an ivory replacement. Zeus punished Tantalus after his death, when he was perpetually *tantalized* with withheld food and drink.

Two of Pelops's sons Atreus and Thyestes went from strength to strength, including but not limited to treason, rape, incest, and murder. The boys also inherited Tantalus's cannibal gene. Atreus, for instance, killed his brother's sons and duped him into eating them. A dysfunctional family. (The useful word "function" goes back to Latin *functus*, done or performed.)

Atreus's own son Menelaus, meanwhile, married Leda's daughter Helen: the most beautiful woman in the world, fathered by Zeus in deep cover as a swan. Yeats describes his rape of Leda as a "shudder in the loins." From Zeus Helen inherited the gene for divine beauty.

When a Trojan, Paris, abducted Helen, Menelaus gathered his Greek peers to help wrest her back. I pass over Paris's backstory as too byzantine (meaning as complicated as Constantinople's politics) to recount. And *byzantine* is the word, since

Troy was *at* ancient Byzantium, the isthmus between Greece and Asia Minor.

The main point of Helen was to give bored Greek men an occasion for *derring-do* ("daring feats").

Also in the mythological stables is the winged horse Pegasus, who helped the youth Bellerophon prove his chops by killing the lion-headed, goat-bodied, snake-tailed, fire-belching *Chimera*. (The *Sphinx*, incidentally, had a similar body type: a lion's body with wings, topped by a woman's head. This particular freak uses strangulation to kill; I believe her name derives from Greek "squeeze," which of course gives us *sphincter* as well.)

Like Pegasus, a horse can be more competent than its master. Take *Balaam's ass*, a biblical donkey who moves to the road's edge to avoid a collision with a bad angel invisible to Balaam. The impatient Balaam whips the donkey, who suddenly gains the power of speech, which humbles Balaam—unfamiliar with *Mr. Ed* and other chatty chargers. Balaam's new humility allows him to view the angel. (Angels, by the way, are men, not women.)

As an aside, *Bible*, like *bibliography*, derives from Greek *biblion*: its plural *byblos* reveals its relation to *papyrus*, "paper."

Before quitting quadrupeds, what exactly *is* an ass? Is it the same as a mule? Who are its parents? What's the thing about sterility? These are questions that keep one awake at night.

Let's lay these questions to rest for good. After some research, I can report that a *mule* is the progeny of a female horse and a male donkey. The (rarer) offspring of a male horse and a *jenny* (female donkey) is a *hinny*. As regards fertility, the male mule is sterile. If, and it's rare, a female mule is fertile, she's called a *molly*. As an *aide-mémoire* you may want to print out this paragraph and post it over your desk or on the fridge.

The *donkey*, or ass, is a *horse of a different color*—metaphorically, because it's *not* a horse—and it adds a level of complexity, so either pay attention here or else familiarize yourself

with the term *pons asinorum* ("asses' bridge"): the level of diffi-
culty where a student's comprehension balks. He throws up his
hands in despair and gives up. A *pons asinorum* is a challenge
that separates true scholars (like Euclid, who coined it) from
dumb asses, unlike Balaam's ass, who was not dumb, being both
astute and talkative. (Note: on this lofty academic plane, the
scholar who can't cross a *pons asinorum* is most likely not a
pathetic dumbass.)

The donkey is cousin to the African wild ass. My research
suggests a portmanteau word derived from *monkey*: *dun*, which
means "gloomy brownish gray" + "monkey." This entire branch
of the genus *Equus*—maligned to the point of libel—should
retain Balaam to litigate in their behalf. The Spanish donkey
is a *burro*, as heard braying and clip-clopping in Grofé's *Grand
Canyon Suite*.

On to horses literally of a different color: Horses come in
special colors dedicated to them alone. (Same with human hair.
Okay, I admit you might talk about furniture's *blond* wood, but
probably you wouldn't describe a house as auburn. You wouldn't
call a car brunette.) See the reaction when you tell the Wedding
Stylist at USA Bridal that you want your bridesmaids in *piebald*
gowns. *Piebald* descends from *pied*, two-colored, like the Pied
Piper and the black and white *magpie* bird who's partial to bling
and goes after anything that glitters.

A *palomino* horse is, likewise, named after a bird: It's ivory-
colored, like "a young dove" (as in Italian *palumbo*, wood-
pigeon). You rarely hear a police APB seeking a six-foot-tall
palomino male in his thirties. Baffle your hairdresser by asking to go *brindle* (from Germanic *bren*, "brown," ultimately from
brennen, "to burn," and a brindled animal does look like something charred on a grill). A *brindle* horse has irregular stripes,
which are the result of *chimerism*—a rare genetic mutation
named after the more-than-mutant Chimera already discussed.

Final and important fact on horses: What about *gee* (say
"jee") and *haw*? These are directional signals used for *all* draft

animals, including sled dogs, so listen up, mushers. *Gee* means turn right; *haw*, left. Unless you're in Britain, where it's the reverse. Chubby Checker agrees, though you may be too young to know the lines from his 1961 song introducing a new dance, *the Pony*:

> Now you turn to the left when I say *gee*,
> You turn to the right when I say *haw* . . .
> Boogety, boogety, boogety, boogety shoo.

By that year, Chubby Checker was an iconic superstar who had already (in 1960) brought to the world a dance phenomenon: *The Twist*. The record went to #1 on the hit parade, stayed on the charts for 16 weeks, and in 2013 topped *Billboard*'s top 100 all-time hits list. The Library of Congress has preserved the recording for "cultural, artistic and historical importance."

So Chubby was *in the catbird seat* (a bird that plies its trade from a perch on the highest branches). Chubby should have been ecstatic. But no: "I was on my way to becoming a big nightclub performer, and 'The Twist' just wiped it out . . . It got so out of proportion. No one ever believes I have talent." (That *talent* started its life as an ancient Greek weight, or a coin of a certain weight. In the Matthew parable, your talents were the valuable things you shouldn't bury.)

Unrecognized talent? Deal with it, Chub. On the other hand, I sympathize with a more recent problem of his. In 2006, Hewlett-Packard and Palm produced a webOS app that used shoe size to estimate penis size—and called the app "Chubby Checker." Checker successfully sued both companies, alleging harm to his "brand and value," and I see his point.

Name-Calling

19

In Name Only

Family Names

In the surnames sector, Britain offers us its own brand of whimsy. Take, for example, the name Gotobed, documented since the Middle Ages and alive today, and so ordinary an activity you wonder why an individual was singled out with the surname. And why is Drinkwater—Boileau in French, Bevilaqua in Italian—so common? As if water drinking is unique to one family. Or possibly the point was that they were teetotalers? Speaking of family: what of *blood is thicker than water*? My Chem I course tells me otherwise. The maxim claims that blood added to water will not form a solution, or even a colloid, but remain an undissolved suspension; i.e., you cannot *dilute* or weaken the tight family bond of consanguinity.

Many family names can be traced back to a particular place. Look at Wales. It's cheek by jowl with England, with Wales in the jowl role, and many common English names are Welsh: Thomas, Williams, Davies, Hughes. Some go back to Celtic origins, like Evans, Morgan, Jones, Owens, and *ap Rhys*, "son of Rhys," which evolved into the surname *Price*.

Re Wales, to anticipate the first-names chapter: Welsh names are spelled funny, to wit *Gwladys* and *Llewelyn*. You can fake Welsh if you write gibberish and throw in a lot of *W*s, *L*s, and *Y*s.

The Welsh national anthem is *Hen Wlad Fy Nhadau*, which the Welsh can probably pronounce and can certainly sing. The Welsh singing voice and Welsh melodies are famous.

Between 1600 and 1800, the Swedes took on many names based on features of nature, such as Bergström (mountain stream) and Lindquist (linden-tree branch). *Vogel* = German "bird." I once knew a girl named *Vogelgesang*—"birdsong." For social/cultural reasons, a family sometimes adopted an *ornamental name*—the official term for a lyrical surname. Names chosen by German Jews include *Rosenbaum* (rose-tree); *Perlmutter* (mother-of-pearl); *Grünblatt* (green leaf); *Einstein* = "one stone." *Bernstein*, linguistic cousin to *brimstone* = "burnt stone"; *Morgenstern* (morning star).

Parenthesis: the Morning Star seen at dawn and the Evening Star (dusk) were once thought to be two different stars. They are one and the same, namely Venus rolling her way across the night sky on her planetary track around the sun. That's her job, since etymologically *planets* = "wandering stars"—which they're not. By the way, an *asterisk* (*) is a "little star."

Talking Shop. You WASPS out there: Your own boring name could be a lesson in industrial and cultural history.

You might descend from someone who made things: Wright, Cartwright, Plowright, Wainwright (wagon-maker), Wheeler, Potter, Turner (lathe-operator), Carpenter, Cooper, Glazer, Saddler, Baker, Cutler (knife-maker), Brewer, Thatcher, Painter, Miller, Mason, to name too many. The front runner is Smith (metalworker), cousin of German *Schmidt*.

Speaking of metals, *plumbers* once worked with Latin *plumbum*, "lead," though today lead pipes outside of the game Clue are no good. Other job titles: Carter, Barker (remover of bark to prepare wood for the Sawyer), Chandler (candle-maker), Faulkner (falconer), Harper, Hunter, Farmer, Fisher, Fowler, Shepherd, Driver/Drover (herdsman), Tyler (roof-tiler), Clark (clerk), and Butler (from "bottler"—the man who serves wine).

You think you know what a hooker is? A *hooker* was a reaper who harvested crops with a reaping-hook. As for prostitutes, *tart* might have begun as a "sweetheart" or a dessert ("sweet tart").

Speaking of carbohydrates, let's consider cereals: A *kellogg* ("kill-hog") was a pork butcher. Regarding pigs, you'd probably guess *Stewart/Stuart* derives from "steward," but did you know that a *steward* was originally a "sty-guard"?

Cloth-workers deserve a detour of a few paragraphs. I spent a chapter above on etymology of clothing and fabrics, which took us to far-flung locations. The focus here is on fabric-related occupations.

Material may have descended from Latin *mater,* "mother." *Matter* is any substance a thing is made from. Latin *materia* can mean "wood." The Portuguese dubbed a chain of islands *Madeira*: "forested."

Full Term. Recall that, like *material, stuff* once had the stricter meaning "fabric" or "cloth." Incidentally, a pair of French stuff(ing) terms: 1) *farci* describes food stuffed with another food and 2) a *farce* began as the "filling-out" of a medieval religious drama with some much-needed comic relief. English derived "fill" from German *füllen,* whence *Gefüllte,* "stuffed," gave Yiddish its *gefilte* fish.

Fulling was old-time fabric-prep. First, you clean your cloth by *fulling* it. One way to full cloth was to wallop the grime out of it with a club. The Romans washed it in large containers of urine where the *fuller* trampled the cloth. The philosopher Seneca described their moves as the *saltus fullonicus* (from *saltus* also recall *somersault,* "to jump upwards/over"). Anyone using kitty litter or diapers knows that urine can smell like ammonia, which has cleansing properties you can test today with, for instance, Rockin' Green Funk Rock Ammonia Bouncer—an "intense cleaning treatment" that's "Biodegradable, Non-Toxic, Cruelty-Free." *Safety tip:* If you mix ammonia and bleach, the resulting fumes can kill you. Workers preferred urine to the alternative, vinegar, which had a stronger odor.

Fulling was called *walking* in Scotland, where the name *Walker* is common (as in Johnnie Walker Scotch): the verb *walk* meant "move around" in general. To lighten the tedium, walkers sang *waulking songs*, stepping up the tempo as the cloth softened. A *waulking* song consisted of stanzas sung by one person and a refrain sung by the whole crowd. Superstition forbade repeating a stanza, but there was a waiver for a refrain. The song tended to be long (like the *ballad*, which, BTW, due to the regular meter, took its name from the *ballare*, "to dance"). Clothwalking continued into the twentieth century.

Interrupting our fabric processes: while we're there, three facts on Scotland:

1) *Scotch tape*: Prior brands, apparently, limited the adhesive to the tape's borders to make it easier to peel off and re-use. Buyers called this design "Scotch," a synonym for "stingy."

2) On *Scotch*, it's mostly better to say *Scottish*, unless you mean the liquor. If you mean the language, it's *Scots*.

3) The Scots were a people more or less synonymous with the Picts; they're referred to in the third century A.D. *Scot* is derived from "shot," which reflects their fierce reputation. The Romans called them the Picts, perhaps describing them as "pictured tribe," for their tattoos.

After fulling, the next step was stretching the fabric on a big *tenter*, a frame to which it was attached by *tenterhooks*. (Latin *tentus*, "stretched," gave us our *tent*.) If you're on tenterhooks, you're experiencing tension.

For woolens, *felting* strengthened wool and helped waterproof it by making it dense. Interested in some hands-on? Martha Stewart provides felting instructions. What I can tell you is this: A knitter friend showed me a mitten sixteen inches long, not as a gift for Tyrannosaurus Rex but to turn into felt by boiling and shrinking it.

Then your material was ready for the *Dyer*. Next it went to the *Draper* (fabric-seller); finally the *Taylor*. Some fabrics went directly to a *Glover*, who used a sewing vise called a *Gloving Donkey*. But your felt you might sell to a *milliner* (hat-maker), derived from *Milaner*, resident of Milan.

Talking Through Your Hat. Making felt hats, however, involved mercury, which gave some felters *mad hatter syndrome*; see Lewis Carroll's *Alice's Adventures in Wonderland.*

As an aside: Carroll, born Charles Lutwidge Dodgson, devised his *nom de plume* (a *plume* was a feather pen) from his real name's Latin form, "Carolus Ludovicus." Speaking of pen names, you probably know how Samuel Clemens found his name in steamboat parlance; *Mark Twain* referred to the second marker in a river-depth gauge (a *twin* is one of twain).

Many hats—Stetson is one brand—are actually made from beaver (or rabbit) fur. The hat-felting process originally soaked beaver fur in camel urine, which eventually was replaced by human urine. Another step might be *carroting* the fur—steaming mercury-coated animal skins to an orange color. Eventually, though, felt hats were made from wool. These included *homburgs* (from the German town) and *fedoras* (after the French drama titled *Fédora*, starring a Russian lady named Theodora).

Syphilitics treated with mercury produced the best urine. But mercurous chloride, as Little Willie (sketched above) proved, is bad for the health. Back in 1860, a Dr. Freeman from New Jersey had already described "Mercurial Disease Among Hatters." Nobody paid any attention: felted beaver pelts were the must-have hat. Not till 1941 did public-health doctors outlaw mercury-felting.

Speaking of which, *doctor* began as a generic term for anyone with a doctorate-level degree, not just in medicine. In Italy, any educated man was addressed as "*dottore*." Italy is also the place where a few surgeons gave the famous and infamous *Medici* family its name.

Other terms of address: Suppose you had only a master's degree. Latin *magister* became "master" and "mister." *Mrs.* abbreviated "mistress," from French *maîtresse*. A lesser (i.e., unmarried) woman, a mere *Miss*, wasn't worth wasting breath on the two syllables of "mistress." Incidentally, a *spinster* was not necessarily an *old* maid. To return to fabric fabrication, spinning was simply one possible job for any single woman with no husband to support her. It became legal language, in fact: a "spinster" was an unmarried woman of any age. The term was used in wedding announcements, where a bride-to-be was a "spinster of this parish."

An honorific that has come a long way is the *esquire* used by American lawyers. In Britain this title is a vestige of the practice where *barristers* (courtroom lawyers), unlike *solicitors* (general-purpose lawyers), were styled "Esquire."

The Christian church generated its own surnames. A *Palmer* was a pilgrim who returned from the Holy Land with a palm leaf—symbolizing Christ's entry into Jerusalem—as testament to his accomplishment. An *Abbott* is CEO of an abbey. Watergater John *Dean* had an ancestor who was a *decanus*, the boss of ten monks. Hollywood's first big-time gossip columnist happened to be a Louella *Parsons*. The poet Anne *Sexton* had a church janitor-cum-caretaker somewhere in her lineage.

The surnames *Cohen* and *Khan*, from Hebrew *kohein*, "priest," were given to the tribe descended from Aaron. The source of *Levy* and *Levine* is the tribe of Levi; during the Temple era, the Levites assisted priests.

You Name It. Some people have special reason to be proud of their surnames. Lucky the individual whose name enters the vocabulary and nets him fame as an *eponym*. And an *eponym* has really arrived when it gains lower-case status.

Take *mesmerize*. Franz Mesmer was born in 1734 in Iznang,

Germany, but naturally gravitated to the happening place where all psych-dudes ended up, namely Vienna. Mesmer came up with the theory of "animal magnetism." (The word *magnet* refers to a kind of rock from Magnesia, on Greece's eastern coast.) Mesmer would have his patients ingest a quantity of iron, and I don't mean merely liver or spinach, and then run a magnet over their bodies, hoping to induce them into a trance. (By the power of suggestion? Who knows?) He later developed a touch-free method, seating them in front of a vat sprouting iron rods and moving his hands and eyes next to this apparatus to "transfer" imaginary fluid to the credulous chump. Mesmer had many disciples, his biggest booster, incidentally, was the agreeably-named Jesuit priest Maximilian Hell.

George Simons invented a wax that *simonized* your car. Sanford Cluett patented *sanforization*, which prevented clothes from shrinking. Also in the domestic arts arena, you *hoover* your floors thanks to "Boss" Hoover, who purchased the patent of a "suction sweeper." This was a family enterprise; his daughter fabricated the vacuum bags. (And don't confuse this Hoover with the 31st US president.) Luigi Galvani, inventor of bioelectricity, sent shocks into test animals and gave us *galvanize*.

More controversial is pediatrician Richard Ferber, who recommended *ferberization*—letting an infant cry for an increasingly long period before responding to it. Thomas Bowdler, prude extraordinaire (who published Shakespeare with vulgarities removed) gave us *bowdlerize*.

Unfortunately, the suffix *-ize* (British *-ise*) can be too much of a good thing. Useful, yes. But it takes an ugly turn with a word like *incentivize* (though that's better than the unspeakable *incent*).

Some proper-names-gone-permanent are pejorative. Consider the Norwegian Vidkun Quisling, Nazi collaborator. A *quisling* is a traitor, as is a *fifth-columnist*, named for soldiers hidden in Madrid (which I claim is from Spanish *madre*) who aided a general marching four columns of troops to attack the city.

Judas, of course, was the quintessential traitor. Some say the *judas tree* is the species on which Judas hanged himself; others think it's named for its flowers, said to carry a toxin that tricks bees to pollinate it. A *judas window* is a window for spying.

A herdsman could tell you that a *Judas-goat* is a frizzy agent in the field who befriends sheep and lures them to the slaughter-pen. The *bellwether*, on the other hand, is a sheep wearing a bell who leads the herd home to the cozy fold. *Bellwether* evolved into any indicator of a trend, where *indicator* means pointer, as in *index* finger.

Some eponyms are useful but unhealthy—although I guess it's an honor to be a disease. It must have been Hansen's dream-come-true to become leprosy. Same for Daniel Salmon and *salmonella*. Ditto Parkinson, Asperger, and Alzheimer. *Ditto* (Italian) = "(already) said."

20

On a First-Name Basis

To Name Names

We already know *Margaret* as "a pearl." And not only a pearl, but a cousin of *margarine*—named for its pearly appearance.

Some names sound ugly till you learn what they mean. *Barbara* sounds like a babbling baby. That's because it derives onomatopoetically from "stutter" and came to mean the language of "barbarians." Barbara redeems itself by meaning "exotic, foreign, barbaric," adjectives you could apply to *Barbie*. Anyway, I know half a dozen human *Barbara*s, and there's not a dud in the lot—okay, maybe one—and even she isn't that bad. (A *barb*, by the way, from *barba*, is a beard-shaped object.)

History has come up with some God-awful Christian names (as given names were called in some cultures). My ancestors include not only a pile of *Patiences* and a *Grace* Crackbone, but also a *Wait* Simpson and a *Waiting* Robinson (as in: let's get through this unpleasant life and get to heaven ASAP), plus a *Thankfull* Robinson, gratitude hanging heavy on his shoulders.

Some currently-common names have unfortunate Biblical meanings. I give you the perpetually curious *Michael*, for example: *Michael* is interrogative; it actually signifies, "Who is like God?" His name is a *question*? Other Hebrew options: *James* = "a heel." It also denotes "he who undermines," if you like that any better. *Joseph* = "he will add" (better than subtract, I suppose).

Theodore = Greek, "God-given"; *theo* = "god" in Greek. The word evolved into Latin *deus,* as in Mozart's baptismal name, Johannes Chrysostomus Wolfgangus Theophilus. His name is a polyglot mishmash: *Johannes* and *Wolgang* ("wolf's journey") are German. Greek *Chrysostomus,* "golden-mouthed," is the right word for a composer. (*Stoma* means "mouth"; hence *stomach.* But not in *colostomy,* where *-tomy* means "cut out." An *a-tom* is a thing that can't be cut into smaller pieces. Even a *tome* originates in a section cut from a larger book.)

But who says a name has to mean something? Make up your own. *Jayden* and *Caden,* for example, placed in the leading 11 boy names for 2014, with *Kayden* at #57 and *Zayden* at #75. Blame the long-popular Gaelic *Aidan* ("fiery"), running at #4 or #5 on the 2020 list. Not that all the names topping the list are invented; among that year's 100 most popular baby names: *Saint, Atlas, Tennessee, Dune,* and *Kale.*

Kale's female counterpart is *Romaine* (63rd spot). *Brooklyn* (#9) and *Ireland* (#76) place well; *Chelsea*s and *Brittany*s are older favorites. *McKenzie* has had a good run (in the top 60 girls' names for four recent years), noting that you often give it the most preposterous phonetic spelling you can come up with.

Luckily, modern culture has brought much-needed variety to given names in English-speaking regions—luckily because the field was once pretty limited. For a while there (centuries, in fact) we were heavy on *Elizabeth*s and *Mary*s, the latter often shortened to *Molly* or *Polly* by the same bewildering process where *Margaret* becomes *Meg* or *Peg*; and why aren't Elizabeths called *Egg*?) Same with boys' nicknames: *Dick* comes from *Rich* from *Richard*; *Bob* from *Rob* from *Robert.* But why must an *Edward* be *Ned* or *Ted*? What about *Ded*?

Discussed above under religion, *Mary* (Maria, Marie) was long #1, as reflected in Mother Goose—full of Marys who, due to vagaries of rhyme, are contrary or mind the dairy except when followed to school by a lamb providing much hilarity at recess.

In case you don't know Mother Goose from a mongoose:

Mary's male counterpart is *John*, who inanely and nightly goes to bed with one shoe off and one shoe on; the same Johnnie who tomcats around at the fair while his girl wails *Oh, dear, what can the matter be?* (She should just dump him with a *Dear John letter.*) Johnnie's the sad lad telling the rain, rain, to go away because he wants to play, and where are *Fantasy Football* and *Fortnite* when he needs them?

Jack is a nickname for John, and its use in *Mother Goose* is statistically significant: There's obnoxious Little Jack Horner ("What a good boy am I!"). There's scrawny Jack Spratt, whose tastes in food complement his fat wife's. Jack accompanies Jill uphill, bad idea. He's nimble at the candlestick-vault, but he's the slacker who gets the sack in *See, saw Margery Daw.*

Anyway, I say call a girl something *mellifluous* ("flowing like honey"). Maybe even *Melissa*, which actually *means* "honey"; *Deborah*, "bee," lacks Melissa's fluent grace, though porno-cheerleader Dallas-Doing Debbie did her bit to liven it up by living it up.

What's in a name?

I'll tell you what. A lot, in my experience: Spell my name Debra, you get a fast trip to the Inferno, and not an outer circle either, and no time for the psychopomp to arrive. *Deb* is marginally better than *Debbie*, but it was a poor choice for the salesman who hoped to sell me a car.

I don't mind quite so much when the vet, addressing my dog, refers to me as "Mom"—she's not really calling me a bitch.

21

Talk of Many Things:
Cabbages—and Kings

Pedigree and Politics

This chapter concerns affairs of state, but to justify its title, three cabbage facts. 1) Cabbage is an "Elixir for Baldness." 2) Record cabbage size (1865): 123 pounds. 3) The late 1970s spawned some freaks known as Cabbage Patch Kid dolls, "soft-sculpted Individual Artworks". . . At the height of this fad, stores had to hold lotteries to determine purchasers, fistfights broke out between potential customers, and police were called to help quell "near riots." Competition was literally cutthroat: One Texas customer realized "another shopper's purse strap was wrapped around her throat."

I've been rambling on about family names. Now several pages on kinship terms.

Pedigree originated in the French *pied de gru*, "crane's foot." Implausible, maybe, but it's a medieval term for what the branches on a family tree look like.

Less and less does anyone give a rodent's rump who your family is. It hasn't always been so. In many cultures your identity was—even now is—your ancestry.

By the Middle Ages, if you were a European noble inheriting an estate, your name was your land. You were "Richard of Southmorland" or just plain "Southmorland." In Shakespeare, people even refer to a king as simply "France" *tout court* or "Norway," as in "Norway, uncle of young Fortinbras."

Surnames denoting your ancestor's appearance are obvious: Black, White, Gray, and the founders of publishing house Little, Brown and Company.

Your name carried a lot of (preferably good) ancestral baggage. If your surname didn't refer to a fiefdom, town, trade, or appearance, it might be simplest to know you as your father's child. Peter*son*. *Mac*Leod. *O'*Brien. *Fitz*patrick, (distantly) from Latin *filius*, "son."

Other cultures take kinship even more seriously, and they have the words to show it.

With in-laws, Latin differentiated your siblings' spouses from your spouse's siblings. A Roman had both an *amita* (paternal aunt, the root of our "aunt") and a *matertera*, maternal aunt. The corresponding uncles: *patruus* and *avunculus* ("little ancestor," i.e., "uncle"). We derive our all-purpose English *cousin* from Latin *consobrinus*, "mother's sister's son," which is based on *soror*, "sister."

Sometimes English has relatively few subtleties and distinctions: our word *man* takes on shades of meaning depending on the context; but still, a man is a man. Latin sports two *men*: A *vir* is a man with honorable qualities, "virtue" or manliness. A *homo* is a biological *human*—from "humus." In Genesis, the first physical human is *Adam*—Hebrew, "created from dust."

In a debate, an *ad hominem* argument attacks the man, not the argument. Here I'll interrupt the program for a few other Latin abbreviations:

i.e. = *id est* (that is)
etc. = *et cetera* (and other things)
e.g. = *exempli gratia* (for example)
et al. = *et alii* (and other people) or *et alia* (other things)
ad lib = *ad libitum* (however you desire)
ad hoc = for this (specific reason)

Watch out, though. In *homosexual*, *homo-* also means "one" or "same": *homogeneous*, *homonym*, and a lot of science words we can ignore.

In the kinship-lingo department, the Russians make the Latin system look simple: The term for your "great uncle" depended on whether he was older or younger than your grandparent. The Russians, of course, are a showcase for *patronymics*, where your (gender-ended) middle name represents your father (Petro*va*, Petro*vich*).

In France, the *Caroli*ngian line began with Charles Martel ("the Hammer"). This family included: Charles the Fat, Charles the Bald, Pepin the Short, Pepin the Middle, Pepin the Hunchback, and Childebert the Adopted. Vividly unambiguous.

Even in democratic America, political dynasties (*dyno* = powerful) are sprouting like Hydras (Kennedy, Clinton, Bush). We need catchy monikers to distinguish members of families. Bush I and Bush II lack luster, nor do "H.W." and "W." (nor even the folksy and Russian-like "Dubya") add dignity. And it's not as if we have no options. Examples include:

1) Roman historians Pliny *the Elder* and Pliny *the Younger*;
2) French father-and-son authors Dumas *père* and Dumas *fils*;
3) Venero *"Benny Eggs"* Mangano, Vincent *"Ace"* Mangano, Lawrence *"Dago"* Mangano, and Philip *"The Rat"* Mangano;
4) brothers at an English school: Smith *Major* and Smith *Minor*;
5) the aforementioned Carolingian model: Holy Roman Emperor Frederick *Barbarossa*, distinguished from the other Fredericks by his *red beard*. William the Conqueror's son William *Rufus* (red-faced) was the beginning of a veritable William-rainbow: William III was William of Orange.

Parenthetically, with regard to dynastic characteristics, German royalty can advance our study of *cephalometrics* (head measurements). *Prognathism*—a jutting chin—is known as the *Habsburg jaw*; there's also the *Austrian lip*. Unfortunately, abundant inbreeding in Europe's royal intermarriages ensured perpetuation of the gene.

Ditto *hemophilia*, once called *the royal disease* (not to be confused with the medieval scrofula known as the *King's Evil*, which was *cured* by the monarch): Queen Victoria was a hemophilia carrier, and her descendants strewed it all over Europe, where it made itself at home, especially in Russia. I'm partial to the literal meaning of *hemophilia*: "love of blood." Western Europe gave Russian royals *czar* and *tsar*—from "Caesar" (as is German *Kaiser*).

Leaving genetics, consider an earlier English king with other problems. Long before Victoria's reign, the British nobility had reined in the monarchy with the *Magna Carta* (1215), where King John was a real loser. For one, he lost (to France) the English duchy Normandy. The Normans called him, *Johan sanz terre*; in Britain he was "John Lackland."

The nobles might not have ganged up on John if he'd hired an *ombudsman* (from Swedish *justitieombudsmannen*, the officer who fields grievances about injustices).

Anyway, the "Great Charter" granted the aristocracy a number of rights.

Right is always the good side, inevitable in a world where human right-handedness dominates. At least as early as the Upper *Paleolithic* ("prehistoric stone" age), more right- than left-handed people just happened to live long enough to pass the trait on to their offspring.

Speaking of hands: When the earliest human, *homo habilis* ("handy man"), no longer spent his time dangling from a branch, one thing he could really use was a serviceable hand. So he grew an opposable thumb to help manipulate objects, and he became quite *dextrous*—spell it *dexterous* if you like—where *dexter* = right (hand).

Latin *dexter* evolved into French *droit* and our *adroit*. "Right" often means "morally right." *Dieu et mon droit* ("God and my right") is the motto on the British royal crest. A right is a pre-

rogative, as listed in the Bill of Rights. The political *right* dates
to the *Parlement* ("speaking place"), where during the French
Revolution you sat on the right if you favored preservation of
the *Ancien Régime*.

For cynics, *might makes right*. A feudal lord, for instance,
allegedly enjoyed the *droit du seigneur*, or *jus primae noctis*
("right of the first night"), which meant first sexual dibs on any
bride married on his estate—he comes even before the groom.

The wedding-night entitlement, while rare, survived up to
the Industrial Revolution. Most often it occurred *de facto*, not
de iure—"in effect," not "in law"; a patrician seduced a parlor
maid, who, when she got pregnant, married a man of her own
class. The epitome of *de facto* might-makes-right is a sovereign
defending his power as *the divine right of kings*, which goes like
this: "I'm sitting on this throne because God put me here."

Last word on right-ness. Sailors need boatish parlance.
Originally, the guy in the stern steered the canoe with his paddle in his right hand. As watercraft developed, the "steer-board"
remained on the *starboard* side.

Left = badness. The Latin word *sinister* means "at your left
hand." *Gauche* is French for "left." It's unlucky to walk around a
church *widdershins*—counterclockwise. The term derives from
old German *wedder*, related to our "wider," and *sinnen/sind*,
"travel," which is a cousin of our "send." (Buddhists, meanwhile,
show respect by walking clockwise.)

A *bar sinister* on your family crest denotes bastardy somewhere. When dukes are helping themselves to peasant girls,
there's going to be progeny out of wedlock, where *wed* derives
from Latin *vas, vadis*, "legal guarantee." Of course, if a duchess
fails to produce an heir, one of those uppity bastards might go
after the patrimony. To preserve the family bloodline, he can
ask the king to legitimize him so he and his descendants can
become genuine aristocrats. *Genuine* is the right word. It derives
originally from Latin *genu*, "knee": a baby's father took the baby
in his lap to guarantee he'd sired it.

Then there's the *left-handed marriage* where, at the altar, the bride was offered not the groom's right hand but his *left*. Oh, the *humiliation*. This was also called a *morganatic marriage*, from the *Morgengabe* or "morning-gift" the husband gave his wife the morning after the wedding night. The custom prevented the permanent taint of a royal family with substandard blood. When a high-status husband wed a social inferior, a morganatic marriage excluded her and their children from getting his title or inheritance, which could only descend to the legal offspring of another marriage. Take that, gold-diggers.

Straight Talk. Even in our enlightened era, some think the institution of marriage has its limits. Single-sex marriage apparently threatens the institution of wedlock: you can't have mobs of gay couples gunning down "traditional" families all over the place.

Fighting Words. So much for the "pedigree" in the chapter heading—which also mentions politics; and for lack of a better spot, here I'll shoehorn war into the text.

The term *jingoism* (aggressive patriotism and willingness to go to war), sprang up with a late-nineteenth-century British ditty: "We don't want to fight but by Jingo if we do, we've got the ships, we've got the men, we've got the money too." *By jingo* is a euphemism for "by Jesus!"

Jingoists are given to *saber-rattling*, which I mention so I can report a nice malapropism recently heard on the radio: *sable-rattling*. Heads up, PETA.

Those previous jingoists are today's hawks, who often have no trouble finding a *casus belli*: a cause of, or justification for, war. For example:

1) Spaniards boarded the ship of a British Captain Jenkins and cut off his ear. The ear was shown to Parliament (1739) and became the *casus belli* for the eighteenth-century *War of Jenkins' Ear.*

2) In Iraq, Saddam Hussein's alleged "weapons of mass destruction" were a *casus belli* for Operation Desert Fox. À propos of toxic chemicals, the original "Desert Fox" was German field marshal Erwin Rommel of North Africa, who killed himself with cyanide on Hitler's orders.

At a Loss for Words. In the eponymous *Pyrrhic victory*, third-century Greek king *Pyrrhus* beat the Romans—*but* at a huge cost, lending his name to a win with heavy losses. Other Pyrrhic victories: At Borodino in Russia (1812) Napoleon lost two thirds of his army. In the 1916 Battle of the Somme, France and England won six miles of ground—ground where almost 150,000 men died, with more than 19,000 British killed on the first day. Although the British routed the colonists at Boston's Battle of Bunker Hill (1775), the Redcoats suffered roughly two times as many casualties as the colonists. It was at Bunker Hill that an American fighter is said to have ordered, "Don't shoot till you see the whites of their eyes."

Like sports metaphors, warfare metaphors are legion. Take *vanguard*, which is really *avant-garde*, the front line of troops. *Bullets* alone are items which civilians are always sweating, biting, dodging, and inserting in PowerPoint lists. As Edward Bulwer-Lytton said, "The pen is mightier than the sword" (which some wags have rendered as "the penis, mightier than the sword"). We'll heed his maxim and move on from swords to more words.

22

Talk of the Town

Place Names

Often a city's name conveys its history. Greece colonized much of southern Italy as part of *Magna Graecia*—"greater Greece": before it became *Napoli*, Naples was Greek *Neapolis*, "new city." Also from *polis*: Latin *politicus*, "civic." *Constantinopolis*, Constantine's city, started its career as Greek "inside the city," *eis tan polin*, hence *Istanbul*. *Acropolis* = "high city." Another *-polis* is Superman's adopted home town *Metropolis*, "mother city," from *mater*, "mother."

Back to Naples for a moment: In English, *Neapolitan* describes an ice-cream configuration that was big in the mid-twentieth century: inch-wide stripes of vanilla, chocolate, and strawberry. Napoleon Buonaparte means "big man of Napoli." Unless, and I'd like to hear why, you insist it derives from the *Nibelungen*, mythical German dwarfs. Surely his parents couldn't predict his short stature.

Russia honored her leaders with political city-name flip-flops. In 1914, they changed *St. Petersburg* (*burg* cadged from German) to *Petrograd*. It became *Leningrad* in 1924 and reverted to St. Petersburg in 1991. Volgograd started as *Tsaritsyn*, but Stalin wasn't having any of that, and it became *Stalingrad*. In 1961, Khrushchev officially restored it to *Volgograd* (*-grad*—"land around a place"—is cousin to "yard" and "garden," which poorly describes this industrial city).

What about *Paris*? The giant *Gargantua*, hero of a Rabelais novel, visits Paris, where the crowds irritate him so much that he drowns 260,418 of them in a flood of urine. Whereupon the survivors laugh so much the city is renamed *Par ris* ("in fun"). LOL, for some people.

Compelling as the urine hypothesis may be, *Paris* began as *Lutetia Parisiorum*, after the Parisii tribe the Romans encountered there. Nobody knows where the *Lutetia* part came from, but *lutetium*, Element 71 in the periodic table, was named for Paris, where it was discovered.

Athens' foundation myth recounts a contest between Poseidon and Athena for the title of city patron. Poseidon struck the earth with his trident and water gushed up, wowing the populace of the drought-plagued town. One *snafu* (acronym for *situation negative, all fucked up*, or *fouled up* in polite circles): it was salt water—useless. Athena planted an olive tree that would provide food, oil, and wood. The vote went to her.

When it came to overseas place-names, the insular British had a trick. An example is the Italian port *Livorno*. First they called it "Legorno." But names ending in vowels sounded alien, so they created—*Leghorn*. What *is* a leg horn? An ankle-restraint? A homage to the Roman *tibia*? (*Tibia* = Latin "shin bone," and a *tibia* was also a flute made from a shin bone.) No. What the English needed was two homey, Anglo-sounding, consonant-intensive syllables. *Leghorn* survives as 1) a breed of chicken and 2) a Tuscan straw woven into hats.

The English firmed up other oily Italian names like Napoli (*Naples*). They tidied the sloppy garlicky vowels of Torino and Venezia into *Turin* and *Venice*. Those Italian *Z*s were so foreign; nor did their xenophobic tongues fancy *Firenze*: hence "Florence," which at least evoked the original *Florentia* and *Fiorenze* redolent of flowers.

People and food also got English makeovers: Roman orator *Marcus Tullius Cicero* became the affectionate *Tully*, while the confectionery *marzipane* became *marchpane*.

And Arabic? Forget it. The *Rosetta Stone*, why? Because it was located in *Rashid*, Egypt.

Moving to the US:

The Northwest Territory's governor belonged to the *Society of the Cincinnati* (members were male descendants of Revolutionary War officers). The name honored Roman general *Cincinnatus* ("curly-haired"), who left the army to be an early peacenik. Cincinnati, OH, had been Losantiville—town opposite (*anti*) the mouth (*os*) of the Licking River. Despite all this Latin, the city, a big pig town, later earned the repulsive nickname *Porkopolis*.

Phoenix, Arizona, was christened by Darrell Duppa, a nineteenth-century French pioneer who 1) styled himself "Lord Duppa" and 2) named the new town for the mythical bird that incinerates itself and rises from its own ashes (only one phoenix can exist at a time). A classicist, he called a nearby town *Tempe*, referring to Thessaly's *Vale of Tempe* frequented by Apollo and the Muses.

Some US states went Latin: *Pennsylvania*, "Penn's woods." A few recognize monarchs: there's *Georgia*, and *Virginia* pays tribute to Elizabeth, the "Virgin Queen." *Carolina*, like Lewis Carroll, is Charles, Latinized. *Louisiana* refers to French Louis XIV. *Florida* is the US version of Florence. In naming states, the West used Mexican Spanish geography: *Montana*, "mountainous." *Colorado*, "colored (red)." *Nevada*, "snowy." The *Sierra Nevada* is a snow-covered mountain ridge, jagged or *serrated* from Latin *serra*—"saw."

Back in Europe:

If the florid Italian language unnerved the buttoned-up English, Latin had reached their isle ready-made. The Roman army occupied forts—*castra*—which developed into cities ending in -*caster*, -*chester*, or *cester*. A small military camp, a *castellum*, produced *castles*.

Incidentally, between the twelfth and sixteenth centuries, in order to build a castle, you had to be granted a royal *License to Crenellate*—to install those picturesque roof-ramparts with squared-off gaps for shooting. The king wasn't keen on ambitious quasi-vassals holing up in fortified castles, but a nobles' true concern was defense from his land-grabbing peers, not to mention sundry freelance plunderers.

Every country has its "new castles": France is cluttered with *Neufchâtels*; Italy has probably hundreds of towns named *Castelnuovo*. But the prize goes to the German fairy-tale castle *Neuschwanstein Castle* whose evocative name says it all: "new swan of stone." *Newcastle* in the north of England began as a Roman town built up by Norman developer Robert *Curthose* ("short-stockings") into a new castle. The river Tyne, handy for transport, helped it become a big coal-mining region, spawning the phrase "carrying coals to Newcastle"—i.e., providing superfluous goods.

Villa (a Roman country-house or farm) gave us "village" plus all the *-ville* towns in the world. Attached to a *villa* were feudal farm laborers, *villeins*, or *peasants* (from *pays*, "countryside"), spelled "pheasants" by the occasional student.

A *vicus*, the Latin term for a little civilian town near a Roman fort, is cognate to Anglo-Saxon suffixes *wick*, *wyck*, and *wich*, which you find in English towns that began as Scandinavian settlements, often on England's eastern coast. A Norwegian *vik* is an inlet, and a *Viking* was a person from a fjord. Remote Reykja*vik* was founded by a Norseman. *Reykjavik* = "bay of smoke"; *reyk* is kin to *reek*, "emit smoke (or any odor)." *Norwich* was a "north village." You also have your *Eastwick*, Rhode Island, which, according to John Updike, harbored witches, and your *Sandwich*, a sandy bay and home of the Earl who invented the sandwich. *Bailiwick* = area of jurisdiction.

Another Anglo-Saxon group includes the *dorps*, *dorfs* (*Waldorf*, "forest settlement"), and the *thorpes* and *throps* common in England (*Northrop*, "north village"; *Winthrop*, "wine village"). A number of Yorkshire towns end in *-thwaite* (from old Danish *thveit*, "unwooded area"). These were a convenient target for Norwegian Vikings going *berserk*: Norse *berserker*, "warrior in a bear shirt," was a charitable allusion to their *ruthlessness* (Hebrew *ruth* = "mercy"). As Gene Pitney might put it: when the Vikings came to town, the womenfolk would hide.

In the ninth century, Britain was overrun by Vikings under Ivar the Boneless. He was presumably a vertebrate, so some call the nickname a metaphor for impotence. Modern health professionals might diagnose it as early-onset osteoporosis.

The Great Heathen Army, led by Ivar and his brother Halfdan, conquered northeast Britain—without the help of their brother Sigurd Snake-in-the-Eye. The Roman garrison *Eboracum* became Anglo-Saxon *Eoforwic* ("wild-boar-village"); the Vikings pronounced it "Jorvik" until it finally stopped at *York*. New Yorkers: Raise an etymological glass now and then to Ivar the Boneless.

A *town*, cognate of German *Zaun*, "fence," is one size up from a village and ended up in many a *-ton*. (By the way, the individual who sells stolen goods was called a "fence" because he operated as a de*fence* against detection.)

Haver = "harbor" or "haven." *København* is Copenhagen, a haven for the merchant, "*køber*." Also from *haver*: the *Hague* and *Le Havre*. Speaking of haven, the *shelter* these ports provided descends from an Old English word for "shield."

All the above place-names are *secular*—i.e., temporal, "dependent on time, non-eternal." But thousands of towns grew up around European religious centers.

Latin *ministerium* ("ministry") became *monasterium*. The German form, *münster*—whose umlaut-topped *ü* resembles our English short i—became a *minster* in Britain, where *-minster* cities abound. *München* (Munich), named for its twelfth-century monks (*Mönch*, "monk"), is the capital of Bavaria, land of beer and *lederhosen* ("leather pants"). Tip: Munich in Italian is *Monaco*. Pay attention if you're boarding a train to the miniature country Monaco in southern France, or you'll end up hearing German instead of French.

Lots of English towns are -*churches*. *Church* and -*kirk* (Scots) are cousins to German *Kirche*—which is part three of the expression *Kinder, Küche, Kirche* ("children, cooking, church"), as the Nazis and others defined the (sole) role of women. Speaking of the war and churches, *Dunkirk* across the Channel means "dune-church." The French term for the English Channel, by the way, is *La Manche*, "The Sleeve"; in German it's an arm-shaped channel, *Ärmelkanal*. The sleeve's cuff is the narrow strait between Dover and Calais, with its wider shoulder between Cornwall and Brittany.

A *holm* (like *Stockholm*) is an island, but it has nothing to do with our "home," which is the sibling of German *Heim*. Other members of the *Heim* family include -*ham* and *hamlet*. By the way, Shakespeare's *Hamlet* sounds like a pork cutlet until you know he's actually the Danish *Amleth*. Some sources say *Amleth* descends from an *Amlóði*, a "simpleton," which pretty well describes the Danish prince who couldn't decide whether to be or not to be. I like the theory that it's a Gaelic derivation from the Norse *Olaf.*

Don't confuse -*berg*, "mountain" (an *iceberg* is an "ice mountain") with *burg*, a "fortified place." British Admiral Mountbatten, born *Battenberg*, Anglicized his name during World War I to jettison its German aspect. Despite his title (Lord Mountbatten of Burma), his grandparents' marriage had been morganatic, and instead of a "Grand Ducal Highness," he was only a "Serene Highness"—bummer. He married "Princess Victoria of Hesse and by Rhine," an interesting title with respect to prepositions.

Burg harks way back to the Greek *pyrgos*, "tower." There are -*burg*s all over the US. Not in Britain, though, which instead took on *burg*'s spin-offs *bourgh, burgh, borough, boro,* and *bury*, passing them on to America as well. As for Italy, a *borghetto*, abbreviated as *ghetto*, was a small community outside the city proper. France features *bourg*s; the *bourgeoisie* were the middle class *burghers* of the new towns that grew up in the Middle Ages.

In the Western world, you'll find that your mountains have a preference for *A*: Atlas, Alps, Andes, Apennines, Appalachians, Alleghenies, Adirondacks, and the Atlas range. (In the mountain department, by the way, here's a handy saying: *If Mahomet won't go to the mountain, bring the mountain to Mahomet.* Mohammed ordered a hill to come to him; the hill, summoned, did what my dog does: nothing. Whereupon Mohammed gamely agreed to go to the hill. What a sport.)

Mohammed was pulling the *Canute maneuver.* The Danish king Canute took his throne down to the beach and ordered the tide not to come in. About nature, monarchs were never right. Recall *Xerxes* (probably the Hebrew Ahasuerus, the same who tried to pimp out his wife Vashti): Whatever name we call Xerxes by, not an affable individual and, I'd say, certifiable. When he was bivouacked at the Hellespont, rough seas shattered a bridge over the strait, and Xerxes sentenced the waves to 300 lashes.

To continue my small digression, the ambitious often learn lessons the hard way. We have Damocles, who had the temerity to try out his king's throne, much like Goldilocks, also caught sampling the furniture. Finding Damocles there, the king hung above him a sword held only by a hair. Moral: power = peril.

But our theme was mountains. The *Atlas* range is in northwest Africa. This was home base for the Titan Atlas, who looked at Medusa's snake-haired head and was turned to stone—which for a big guy like him meant a rocky mountain range. He was literally *petrified* into hulks of mountainry. (Note: *Petra* is the Latin for "rock." Hence Jesus' pun when he appointed Simon Peter as the first pope: *Tu es Petrus et super hanc petram aedificabo ecclesiam meam*—"thou art Peter, and upon this rock I will build my church.") He also gave his name to the legendary *Atlantis*, existing (somewhere and supposedly) just west of his domain.

Once, when Hercules was in the area, he broke one of the mountains in half and put the two halves on either side of the Straits of Gibralter—the Pillars of Hercules. The dollar sign used to have *two* vertical lines through the *S* of *US*: $. This symbol is said to derive from the Spanish piece of eight, where the Pillars are pictured and resemble a dollar sign. (A *piece of eight* was an eighth of some amount, a *doubloon* was worth the amount doubled.) There are other theories, though. Some claim the double-lined *S* represented "US," where an *S* was superimposed on a *U* with its bottom erased. Still others say today's $—with only one vertical line—originally stood for "*pesos*."

Gibraltar originated as *Jabal Tariq*, "the mountain of Tariq." Established by the Muslim general Tariq, Gibraltar was ruled by Muslims until 1492. When in Spain, you can also visit two cities founded by Phoenician traders: *Seville* (*sefela*, "a plain") and *Cordoba* (*qorteb*, "oil-press").

So much for mountains (*et al.*).

If you know Somebody Something*ström*, you know he lived near a stream hundreds of years ago. A brook, a *Bach* in German, was a *beck* in England, hence *Steinbeck*, "stony brook." A *beach* is a place at the edge of a *Bach*.

Ponds began as areas encircled by man-made banks, originally not only bodies of water but pens for livestock. Thus *pond* eventually got us to dog *pound*.

Moving to New World waters, here's an example of my quibbling pedantry: *Minneapolis* is a mixed marriage of the Dakota tribe's *minne*, "water," and Greek *polis*, "city." Another example of verbal miscegenation is the Latin *octopi* as plural for Greek *oktopous* (recall Oedi*pus*'s swollen foot). If you don't like "octopuses" or the stilted "octopods" (for whom stilts are hard to picture), neither do I. You can't win.

Now into the woods.

A *forest* (like *foreign*) was "outside [civilization]." *Wood*'s cousin is German -*wald*; the horror that was *Buchenwald* is a "beech wood." On a happier note, the word "book" evolved from *Buch*: beech-wood where runes were carved.

Latin *buxus* morphed into words such as today's "boxwood," "bush," and *Boise*, Idaho (*boisé* = French for "wooded").

Buxus is kin to Greek *pyxis*, "wooden box." And by the way, you should rethink *Pandora's box.* It was actually a 500-gallon stone *jar.* Blame Erasmus, who wrongly translated the text pithos ("ceramic jar") as a wooden *pyxis.* A typical Greek *pithos* could accommodate a lot of evil: supposedly the philosopher Diogenes fell asleep inside one.

Still, despite Erasmus's error, "hope" remained in the box after the horrified girl had slammed the lid down ASAP: We can think of Pandora's box as a kind of hope chest.

But is *hope chest* a happy name for a trunk containing a girl's *trousseau,* the spinster's version of a baby *layette?* (Here let's recall that in England the word "spinster" used to refer to any unmarried woman, however young and comely—not the old maid it came to represent.) The "hope" of *hope chest* seems to imply potential futility; as Dusty Springfield warns, *Wishin' and hopin' and thinkin' and prayin'* won't do a darn bit of good.

Returning parenthetically to *layette,* one must be wary of -*ette* when it's not French. The better class of speaker rejects *dinette, kitchenette, luncheonette,* and *leatherette.*

To return to tree species, the yew-tree (symbolizing death and traditionally found in English graveyards) was Old English *iw,* like your reaction to a corpse dead three days, innards out. Archers used yew for bows.

Regarding trees, and stay with me here, *antimacassars,* the lacy doilies atop easy chairs (not really that attractive), protected the upholstery from *macassar oil,* a men's hair-gel predating even *Brylcreem.* Through the centuries, male shoppers have sought the wet look or hoped to curb a disruptive *cowlick* where a cow might have swiped its tongue across a hank of hair. Macassar was made with flowers of the Indonesian *ylang-ylang* tree. Byron puts the stress on the first syllable and captures it in a handy piece of pentameter: "thine incomparable oil, Macassar."

À propos of personification, a main job of trees is to be people: Isaiah predicts *the trees of the field shall clap their hands.* Not

to mention the trees on Dunsinane Hill. Macbeth gets compla-
cent when a witch predicts "Macbeth shall never vanquish'd be
until / Great Birnam Wood to high Dunsinane Hill / Shall come
against him." In other words, thinks Macbeth, never—until his
foes camouflage themselves as trees.

A biblical finish to the arboreal motif:

1) Noah's ark was built of *gopherwood.*
2) Eden's Tree of Knowledge we always assume was an apple
   tree. Maybe. But Latin *malum* has two meanings: "apple"
   and "evil." Translators might have screwed up.
3) So valuable was *cedar* wood that King Solomon gave Hiram
   of Tyre twenty Galilean towns for a supply of cedar lumber. The two kings formed a mutual merchant marine to
   import gold, silver, ivory, apes, and peacocks from Tharshish. With Josephus, I posit Tharshish was Tarsus which
   is (a) on the southern Turkish coast and (b) on the road to
   Damascus where Saul rebranded himself as Paul. When
   you tour Tarsus, take in Cleopatra's Gate; she entered the
   port in 41 B.C.E., famously (at least to me) described by
   Shakespeare:

> The barge she sat in, like a burnish'd throne,
> Burned on the water: the poop was beaten gold;
> Purple the sails, and so perfumed that
> The winds were lovesick with them; the oars were silver,
> Which to the tune of flutes kept stroke, and made
> The water which they beat to follow faster,
> As amorous of their strokes. For her own person,
> It beggar'd all description: she did lie
> In her pavilion, cloth-of-gold of tissue,
> O'erpicturing that Venus where we see
> The fancy outwork nature: on each side her
> Stood pretty dimpled boys, like smiling Cupids,
> With divers-colour'd fans, whose wind did seem
> To glow the delicate cheeks which they did cool . . .

4) Highbrows treat Joyce Kilmer's ditty "Trees" ("I think that I shall never see / A poem lovely as a tree") with withering scorn, as insipid and over-sentimental. "Poems are made by fools like me, / But only God can make a tree": Creationist, maybe, but the First Amendment does extend to "artistic" expression.

23

Take My Word for It

Malaprops and Mondegreens (A Media Circus)

Now for a break from strict etymology. We can all use a vacation, and it's time for a holiday chapter, by which I mean an overview of two verbal absurdities. As I mentioned in the introduction, these are acquired but not inherited characteristics, nor do they nose their way into our verbal genes. The two phenomena are: the *malapropism*, where the speaker uses a wrong word instead of the (similar) correct one. A *mondegreen* is an aural rather than an oral error; a listener merely *mishears* an expression. But they share several features:

Like the mondegreen, the malaprop commemorates a lady.

Like the mondegreen, it uses real words (it isn't gibberish or Jabberwock).

Like the mondegreen, its result is ridiculous.

You might already know what a malaprop (properly *malapropism*) is, but we'll sample a few recent ones, hot off the press and other media. And a word to the wise, namely journalists, entertainers, politicians, panelists, and interviewees: watch your tongues and your typing. (Not that I myself never blunder, so, reader, let's not exclude you and I, especially if we don't know subject-pronouns from object-pronouns.)

Too few speakers are on speaking terms with English. Perfectly pardonable, except in people who address the public. It's a circus out there.

You may point out, on the subject of circuses, that in an era when the non-PC Fat Lady is history, blooper-shaming is as offensive as fat-shaming. You may say my *de haut en bas* mockery of others' solecisms is pathetic *Schadenfreude*—"harm-pleasure." And also arbitrary; why single out a few purely personal peeves to pounce on? (I plead, with Shylock: *I give no reason . . . more than a lodged hate and a certain loathing.*) Plus, you ask, don't I have anything better to do than smirk over a few harmless gaffes?

But harmlessness doesn't give public speakers a free press pass. Regarding harm, by the way, here (mentioned above) is a sadistic mondegreen: a global-politics maven recently traumatized a totally blameless animal by *sable-rattling.* This individual better find a *saber,* because to my ear those are fighting words. In fact, speaking of journalists and weapons, some writing descends from *free-lances*—mercenary fighters. Anyway, I'm honing my lance-point; and here I'm picking my battles. Malaprops and mondegreens.

Malaprops: Word for Word

You're as likely to hear howlers on an NPR show as on any "lowbrow" program; more likely, in fact. The public-radio pundit fancies himself* an intellectual. He may well be an expert— in his field. So expert, in fact, that his narrow focus ignores vocabulary far-removed from his métier. Once or twice, however, he hears an expression that impresses him. He likes the sound of it. And he tries it out himself. Using it isn't necessarily pretentious. But if it's new to his lexicon, he might end up dropping a malaprop.

The *malaprop* honors a character in Richard Brinsley Sheridan's 1775 play *The Rivals.* Mrs. Malaprop is an appealing ditz

---

*The culprit is equally likely to be female. I use *he* and *him* to avoid the messy gender-neutral alternatives. (Although remember: *they* is now okay.)

who drops big words but uses them *mal à propos*—in the wrong context. Her trademark is substituting an incorrect word for one that resembles it.

Among Mrs. M.'s buffoony mistakes: "He can tell you the perpendiculars." "Promise to forget this fellow—to illiterate him . . . from your memory." "She's as headstrong as an allegory on the banks of the Nile."

Two and a half centuries later, malaprops are alive and well. Prominent people have fallen prey to them. Yogi Berra, allegedly, mentioned Texas's many "electrical votes." A Boston mayor referred to "a man of great statue."

Of the malaprops I've caught on the radio in the last couple of years, I'll quote only a few: this is not a fulsome list, as in, "The agency must conduct a complete and *fulsome* investigation." (How would that work? What does an overly-flattering investigation look like?)

Some actual remarks:

That cake was hardly *palpable*.

They attacked, and the Friday night *reverie* was replaced by chaos. (Describing the 2015 assault by ISIS on a Parisian theatre.)

He was *indefaggotable* in his efforts.

As he droned on, I looked *serendipitously* at my watch. (Aside: the island *Serendivis* inspired Herbert Walpole's 1754 tale *The Three Princes of Serendip* about some youths' fortuitous finds.)

Police are searching for the crime's *perpetuator*. (A serial killer, apparently.)

She *lathered* mayonnaise on her bread. (Flatulence alert.)

Treat an overdose with an effective *anecdote*. (Or choose Narcan.)

I'm *honing* in on a solution. (A solution requiring a very sharp mind.)

We were getting really *exacerbated* by the delay.

I admire his stability—he keeps a steady hand on the *till*.
(Steering the ship with a cash register? Self-confident
robber at a retail store?)
Smoking is *decremental* to your health.
Be careful what you say, or you'll *ostracize* your audience.
(Unclear exactly what word was intended, but *ostracism*
seems counter-productive here.)
A politician represents his *contingency*. ("Constituency"
would sound more optimistic.)

Again, it's public figures by definition (you could say by
wrong definition) whose malaprops we hear most often. In early
2020, CNN reported the Balearic Islands' ruling that anyone
"found flaunting the rules will face fines—in the most serious
of instances, such as the sale of alcohol outside of permitted
hours . . ." (But "flaunting" suggests that the rule-breakers are
parading their non-drunkenness; how do you ostentatiously
display your sobriety?) Merriam Webster sanctions *flaunt*
meaning "flout" on the grounds that it's so commonly used. I
personally believe flouters of the flout/flaunt rule should themselves face fines.

One notorious case was a sort of inverse malapropism: in
a 1999 *cause célèbre*, it was the listener, not the speaker, who
blundered. When a mayoral aide alluded (correctly) to a *nig-
gardly* budget, his colleagues called him on his racist expression. The aide resigned as a result. He shouldn't have caved—he
was rehired after the misperception was explained, and the
NAACP Chairman Julian Bond commented that a speaker
shouldn't have to "censor" his speech to meet other "people's
lack of understanding."

A British judge "*adorns* a wig." (Does he mean "dons"? Or
are we talking ribbons and flowers?)

A New Jersey police chief praised a man who tried to *inter-
dict with* the bad guys. (Seeking papal intervention?)

Speaking of crime, always mistake a more sophisticated

word for the correct one: Cordon off the *parameters* of the crime scene.

Also in New Jersey, a public alert ordered a road closure out of an *excess* of caution. (Blaming his own office for over-reacting.)

Careful using clichés you haven't seen in writing: A WHO official tweeted, "We are in *unchartered* territory with COVID-19." But who *does* rent a pandemic?

And then there's *reticent*. It's everywhere it shouldn't be. A *Wall Street Journal* writer blamed a negligent company for being "reticent to act." Not "hesitant," because why not use the showier "reticent"? I'll tell you why. Because "reticent" means "unspeaking." Recently an NPR panelist commented, in a text-book case of tautology, on "reticence to talk about" a topic. CNN says people are "reticent to go back to work." This fault prevails partly because "hesitant" and "reticent" sound alike and partly because reticence is a *type* of hesitancy: reluctance to *talk*. This particular malaprop has grown roots, spread like a weed, and established itself for good.

When a misuse goes endemic, a *descriptive* dictionary will eventually sanction it: Merriam-Webster's third definition of *reticent* is "reluctant" (note also that in 2019 this dictionary okayed they as a singular pronoun). The more *prescriptive* Oxford English Dictionary on the other hand, forgoes the "hesitant" sense of "reticent." (Maybe you usually use "reluctance" as the ratio of magnetic potential difference to corresponding flux. You still can't use "reticence" in its place.)

So, why do I side with the OED approach, you complain: There's no such thing as "correct" language. You tell me: If words don't change with the needs of the times, why does *etymology* exist, not to mention a book about it? I should try, say, entomology—a little creepy but at least concrete. Today, you point out, we don't speak Shakespeare's English; Shakespeare didn't chat in Anglo-Saxon. Ever since *Homo erectus* got the mental and vocal gear, speech has existed precisely to be intelligible to as many people as is useful. Language evolves, and the planet continues rolling around the sun.

And you're right, except that the errors I quote are exactly *un*intelligible.

Mondegreens: To Coin a Phrase

Where a malaprop is a slip of the tongue, a mondegreen is a slip of the ear. In a day when our information is more likely to come from TV, radio, or podcast than from the page, it's easy to mis-*hear* a word or phrase we haven't seen in print.

A mondegreen doesn't typically trigger a spoken sole-cism. True, you might happen to mention your own wigged-out misperception to someone else, but more likely you merely stow it among the other dusty bagatelles in your mental attic. I'll cite a few misapprehensions I've encountered. First, though, let me introduce Lady Mondegreen.

Yes, modern media give us plenty of opportunity to hear an expression incorrectly. But the eponymous *mondegreen* origi-nates in a seventeenth-century Scottish ballad, *The Bonnie Earl o' Moray*:

Ye heilands and ye lowlands,
O whaur hae ye been?
They hae slain the Earl o' Murray,
And laid him on the green.

American listener Sylvia Wright invented the word (1954) when, as a child, she understood that last line as:

They hae slain the Earl o' Murray
And *Lady Mondegreen.*

Thus died a nonexistent peeress—to be immortalized in the term *mondegreen.* She's an auditory accident.

The mondegreen is like a one-person game of "Telephone" ("Chinese Whispers" or "Russian Gossip" in Britain), where a phrase whispered from person to person in a group devolves into gobbledygook. Or compare it to a spoken phone message transcribed by a computer into enchanting and nonsensical text. Surely you've personally encountered a mondegreen or two, whether the ear-error was your own or someone else's.

You don't need a song, game, or smartphone to mess up a word. *Dramatic*, for example, might be heard as *Germanic*: very different, unless you have Wagner in mind. I know a kindergartner who wrote *tree* phonetically as *chree*.

A generation of teenagers often misheard rock & roll lyrics back when radio reception was fuzzy (enunciation was not the artist's top priority). Sometimes words or phrases can be understood only decades later in remastered versions.

Take just one song (inspired by the title of a preschool drawing by John Lennon's son). One listener heard *Lucy in the Sky with Diamonds* as *Lucy in Disguise with Diamonds*. And remember, the year was 1967: We were talking LSD; consider the song's gorgeous image of "the girl with kaleidoscope eyes." This same phrase spawned a less lyrical but truly dazzling mondegreen, becoming "the girl with colitis goes by."

Yes, some Beatles mondegreens are corporeally unpleasant. Start with "Eleanor Rigby picks up the rice" and get "Eleanor Rigby picks up her eyes." What with the church setting, what we have here is a tribute to the blind martyr St. Lucy, who holds her own eyes on a golden plate. Another Beatles case: in an era when STDs were known as VD, a friend of mine heard not "Lady Madonna" but "VD Madonna," evoking the individual also known as "Round John Virgin."

And it wasn't only the Fab Four. A listener understood the Notorious B.I.G. lyric "I just love your flashy ways" as "I just love your fleshy waist." And an internecine mondegreen: Cass Elliot of The Mamas & the Papas sang "I *began* to pray" where Michelle Phillips had written "I *pretend* to pray."

Surely the ballad that spawned and killed Lady Mondegreen was sung rather than recited. But her namesake mistake is not limited to musical lyrics, nor to words heard on radio or recordings.

A subclass of the mondegreen—not usually exposed until someone writes it down—is the *eggcorn*, a mondegreen that is somewhat logical: an "acorn" was the kernel of an egg-shaped object, "an eggcorn." Speaking of corn, a very recent mondegreen is *corn teen* (variant *corn-and-teen*) for "quarantine." Additional auditory errors that make a sort of sense:

> He suffered from "acid *reflex*." (*Reflux* probably is a kind of reflex.)
> If that's what you think, you've got another *thing* coming. (A *think* is a weird noun anyway. Still, "some*thing* coming" has a soupçon of the ominous about it.)
> A *world wind* sounds like a global cyclone.

But most are absurd:

A seamstress, asked to make a very loose slipcover, replied: "Oh, yes, *shabby-chic*," which her customer heard as *chubby cheeks*. And pathetic fallacy or not, why *shouldn't* an armchair have chubby cheeks?

A mondegreen can go permanent, especially one that's difficult to correct because its source is a foreign language. The Italian sunflower *girasole* became the *Jerusalem* artichoke, a tuber so hideous as to be best left behind in the weird-produce section of the supermarket—but apparently tasty. Another green mondegreen stems from the *rhododendron*. Its roots are Greek (*rhodon* = rose; *dendron* = tree), but I've heard *rhododendrum*: more temptingly Latinate, and wrong.

Speaking of Latinate, consider the appealing *mumpsimus*: OED, "a traditional custom, obstinately adhered to however unreasonable it may be." According to Erasmus, a priest mangled *Quod ore sumpsimus, Domine* ("what we have received in our mouths, Lord"), saying *mumpsimus*; he stuck to it even after he was faulted.

Young children often come up with pleasing mondegreens. A laundry *hamper* is a "vampire." *Déjà vu* becomes "day job view." A *statue* is a "pistachio." (*Statue*, always troublesome— recall the Boston mayor.) You go to *hell in a ham-basket* which, despite any unintended slur on our porcine brethren, would work just as well as a hand-basket unless you require a kosher or halal conveyance.

Students are all about mondegreens. One girl wrote *Golda Meir* as *Golden My Hair.* Another one took something for *gran- ite*—not a bad metaphor, since taking it for *granted* might sug- gest it's "carved in stone." Then there's "there *before* the grace of God." Like "there *but for* the grace of God," her version does imply the deity's blessing, but it lacks the key notion of a mis- fortune avoided.

I hate to single out NPR yet again, but it's rife with (or as some say, *ripe* with) mondegreens:

"He favored bringing the power of the NRA to *kneel.*" Nicely dominating, but the speaker wanted "bringing to *heel*"—com- manding a dog to walk at one's heel.

Then there's the commentator who asserts, "It's a private business that can ban customers at their own *leisure.*" (Right, what's the rush? It beats the actual expression, "at their own *pleasure,*" which evokes a capricious, even captious, feudal king, possibly sadistic.)

Moving way down the feudal org chart, what of the poor serf with a *hard road to hoe*? His task will be tough indeed; a *row* to hoe is laborious enough.

Finally, the occasional mondegreen is a non-word. An acquaintance wrote me that she was becoming *yancy.* Still, although *yancy* has a certain charm, "antsy" is more graphic.

I'll end, as a tot recently said, quickedy-split.

In So Many Words

24

Take a Number

Let's move to numbers.

We begin with *zero*, which derives, like *cipher*, from Arabic *sifr*. (Luckily, because it would pall after a while, we can't go as far as *infinity*, otherwise known as ∞, a symbol which started as an *ouroboros*, a coiled snake eating its own tail.)

I couldn't reach infinity, even if I were *talking nineteen to the dozen*, defined by dictionaries as "to speak rapidly and without stopping." One theory holds that the phrase originated in eighteenth-century Cornwall, where, fueled by a mere twelve bushels of coal, a steam engine in a flooded tin mine pumped nineteen thousand gallons of water. (Mining technology is not my expertise, and these are deep waters indeed, but evidently this statistic was considered impressive.)

But let's pause at *six*, a number prominent among idioms. The mythological sea monster Scylla wears six howling dogs' heads. This lady should definitely be *deep-sixed*, which you do to something unwanted by dropping it six feet (a *fathom*) underwater. Or sinking it all the way to the sea floor, i.e., to *Davy Jones' Locker*, named for the seventeenth-century pirate David Jones.

Which raises the specter of the *Jolly Roger*—the pirate's iconic skull and crossbones. Although a *Jolly Roger* was a term for a jovial man, it became something more sinister in the early eighteenth century. One possible origin of the pirate motif involved

John Quelch, who flew what he at first called the "Old Roger"—
another of the devil's pseudonyms. Others attribute the name
to Bartholomew Roberts, known more colorfully as Black Barti.
Black, maybe, but he wore a scarlet coat, for which the French
nicknamed him *Le Joli Rouge*, which the English heard as "Jolly
Roger." A similar theory: the Tamil pirate Ali Raja became
"Jolly Roger."

Aside: to *roger* a woman (British, outmoded) is to have sex
with her. The expression *have sex with* showed up only in the
last few decades, and it's not much of an improvement over
sleep with, which doesn't cut it even as a euphemism; it's not
about sleeping. Go with *go to bed with* instead. As for the phrase
"Roger that," *Roger* in the military phonetic alphabet was the
letter *R* (for "received").

Before leaving *fathoms*: Today we (by which I mean media
analysts expounding on various issues) use the phrase *sea-
change* freely for every major transformation, but its source
is as marine as it sounds—*The Tempest*, "Come unto these yellow sands."

> Full fathom five thy father lies;
>   Of his bones are coral made;
> Those are pearls that were his eyes:
>   Nothing of him that doth fade
> But doth suffer a sea-change
> Into something rich and strange.

(Incidentally, in another actually marine sea-change, a seal
when on dry land can become a *selkie*—a beautiful, human, and
temporary woman.)

Speaking of *six*'s properties and superstition: Though 666
was the Number of the Beast, it also has its place in mathemat-
ics as 1) a Smith number, 2) the repeating numbers of the magic
total of a prime reciprocal magic square, and 3) in "recreational
math" a *repdigit*, portmanteau of "repeated digit." You can rec-

ognize it as: base B of the number $xB^y - 1$ where $0 > x > B$. No doubt you're already familiar with these terms, so I won't insult you by explaining them.

Anyway, the ocean and Satan can team up to put you *between the devil and the deep blue sea,* or *between a rock and a hard place.*

That's where *Scylla* and *Charybdis* reside. The HQ of this pair was the Straits of Messina between Sicily and Italy. On one coast looms Scylla, a six-mouthed ogress. On the other shore lurks Charybdis, a twelve-tentacled, flipper-footed monster based under a fig tree. She's a whirlpool that really sucks. Their eponymous dilemma forces you to decide which monster is the lesser evil.

Sometimes, even worse, you have *Hobson's choice*—a choice that's no choice at all, as in "You can paint a barn any color you want as long as you paint it red." Hobson, a British livery-stable proprietor, gave horse-renters a "choice": they could hire either the horse in the nearest stall or none.

In the US, *livery* mostly refers to livery cabs. London today, however, boasts 110 "livery companies." The above-mentioned Worshipful Company of Bakers is not alone. *Worshipful Companies* are relics of medieval craft guilds; to this day they regulate aspects of their trades.

Of the Great Twelve City Livery Companies, the Worshipful Company of Skinners (skin-and-fur trade) ranked sixth in precedence in an annual barge procession until 1484 when, due to its violent rivalry with the Merchant Taylors' Company, the Lord Mayor awarded the Taylors the sixth slot in odd-numbered years. Many trace *at sixes and sevens* to this dispute (flaw: Chaucer used the expression a century earlier).

Lower-status Companies include Fishmongers, Makers of Playing Cards, and at #108, the Worshipful Company of Security Professionals.

25

Prison Terms

Security professionals bring us to prisons. How much can I say about jail-related etymology?

About three pages.

There's also *peri*-prison vocabulary (where *peri-* means "around")—in this case pre- and post-incarceration.

His Word Is His Bond. I'll start with one word: *parole* which means "word" in French. A paroled prisoner gives his *parole d'honneur*—"word of honor" to behave himself.

Parole derives from the Greek *parabola*, "a curve," literally "throwing alongside." *Parabola* also evolved into *parable*—a roundabout metaphorical story for the purpose of comparison; recall the parable of the talents above. I've mentioned *hyperbole*: "a throwing beyond." The famous *Discobolus* (fifth century B.C.E.) is the "Discus-thrower." A clearer definition of parabola: *the locus of points such that the distance to the focus equals the distance to the directrix.*

To return to our topic (prisons), I'll throw in a comment on religious penalties. *Shrift* was confession of sins plus penance for them, especially when it meant beginning your sentence without delay. Today, when someone rates little attention, you give him *short shrift.*

Con yields us two crime terms. An *ex-con* (former *convict*) might also have been a *con man* ("confidence man")—a swindler taking advantage of people who trust him.

The *sheriff* as American frontier lawman began his life as an English legal officer, the *shire-reeve*. (Robin Hood had dealings with a particularly pestilent one.) We mustn't leave *reeve* without acknowledging the *hog-reeve*, the eighteenth-century New England officer responsible for dealing with property damage from stray pigs. Another policing professional was the British *bobby*, named after Robert Peel, who created London's Metropolitan Police.

The police car, too, has come by some adorable epithets: *panda car*, for its typical paint scheme, or the even cuddlier *fuzzmobile*. (Why *fuzz*? Some ascribe the term to the fuzzy material of English policemen's helmets. Others claim it's an American mondegreen, and I hope you've done your vocabulary homework, for "feds" or possibly "fuss." Take your pick, or don't bother.) A van for prisoner transport was called a *paddy wagon*. American cops were once mostly Irish, and "Paddy" was short for "Patrick." An opposite theory has "Paddy" referring to the mostly-Irish persons arrested by the New York police. The vehicle was also known as a *Black Maria*, a tribute to Maria Lee, a black woman who in the 1820s ran her boarding house so rigorously that the police used her to capture villains.

In the early 1900s, as later heard in TV westerns, the local jail was the *hoosegow*, from Spanish *juzgado*, "law court"—from Latin *judicatum*, "judgeship." A similar example: *vamos* ("let's go") initiated our nineteenth-century *vamoose*. Today, it's a nice bonanza that *pen* (short for *penitentiary*, a "place to repent") just happens to mean "enclosure." And what about *stir* (as in *stir-crazy*)? Does it descend from Romani *stardo* ("imprisoned")? Damned if I know.

Correctional facilities today go in for some very flashy security technology; no one remembers the medieval *oubliette* ("forgotten place"): a deep vertical dungeon beneath a trap-door. A pity, because what I look for in a prison is old-fashioned picturesque charm.

To trace the word "jail," go way back to Latin *cavea*, as in "cave" or "cavity." A cave would often serve as the local lock-up. This became *caveola* (by the old *-ol/-ul* diminutive), which (by the *v/b* toggle) then became the medieval *gabeola*, then *gaole*, then Old French *jaole*.

Wait. How did the hard *g* of *gabeola/gaole* become the soft *g* of *jaile*? Obviously another case of lazy French tongue: why trek all the way back to your throat to utter a hard *g* when your tongue helps you voice it at the roof of your mouth without breaking a sweat? (Just so you know, I'm a staunch Francophile, and all my jabs at the French tongue are tongue-in-cheek.)

Another example of French *g*-to-*j*: Balking at the hard *g* in *Hrothgar* (Beowulf's king in the Anglo-Saxon poem), the French slid it into *Roger*, which I've already covered *ad nauseam*, except to say that the name means "handy with a spear." Consider the name Hrothgar for your next son—just an idea.

Normandy, on the other hand, hung onto *gaole*. The hardy Norman throat also handled Latin *gamba*, "leg," no problem. Normans ate not *jambon* but *gambon*—"ham," which is the pig's rump, which is why our back thigh muscle became the *hamstring*. Ex-geezers now dead used to call legs *gams*, invariably preceded by "shapely." In the rest of France *gamba* (as in the cello-like *viola da gamba*) suffered the same fate as *gaole*, evolving into *jambe* and *jambon*. By the way, *bacon* = the "back-meat."

Those Normans took "gambon" to England, where the English caved to their own mouth-sloth; but instead of shifting the hard *g* to the tongue and palate as a *j*, they slid it a couple of centimeters down the throat from their British "gammon" into the *h* of *ham*.

Hard *g* is a *guttural* sound (Latin *guttur*, "throat"). Do not use the word like the radio interviewee who mentioned her "guttural instinct." Go with your *gut*, as she did not.

We've gotten away from jail. Aboard ship, you're locked up in the *brig*, a term from the mid-nineteenth century. A square-rigged *brigantine*, when too old to sail, could be used as a prison ship—an Alcatraz afloat with a perimeter fence made of ocean.

The British called it a *hulk*. This hulk was not a musclebound humanoid and definitely not comic-book material. Dickens described hulks in a novel that schoolkids used to label the *Big Spit*, as in *Great "Expectorations."*

Dickens and the sea introduce us to the *caul*—the membrane containing the amniotic fluid around a fetus. Occasionally an infant is born with this item draped around his head. *Caul*'s source is Latin *galea* ("helmet") probably from Greek *kalux*, "case" (in botany a bud is encased in a *calyx*). Be that as it may, David Copperfield was born with a caul, which was supposed to make you undrownable. I don't know whether he ever tested its efficacy.

À propos of *infant*, it literally means "non-speaking" (Latin *infans*).

À propos of *fetus*: *effete* meant "worn out by childbirth"; it evolved into "non-robust" in a more general sense.

Final note on incarceration: Where other than England would you find a men's prison called Wormwood Scrubs? It was built on Wormholt Scrubs, *scrubs* being stunted shrubs. Inmates rate this prison 3.4 stars.

26

Pay the Piper, Call the Tune

I'm done with crime etymologies. But a few pages on my favorite crook, who was a musician. In the early seventeenth century, the verb "sing" was first used in the sense "to rat out"; and although my villain's music was instrumental, not vocal, we can't mention rats without touching on the Pied Piper.

The *Pied Piper of Hamelin* sounds nicer in English than the German *Rattenfänger von Hameln*; still, the man *was* a ratcatcher and only plying his blameless trade as a pest-control professional in a polychromatic suit. And Hamelin town, on grounds currently obscure, refused to pay his fee for ridding the city of rats. Stiffed and miffed, he retaliated for breach of contract with not a lawsuit but a mass abduction.

Hameln should have paid up. It hated its rats: it had a number of flour mills and for all I know still does; in fact, as recently as 2012, a mill closed in Hameln due to market glut. *Glut*, as in "glutton," derives from Latin "to swallow." Greek *glot* gives us *epiglottis* (*epi-*, "near" + "tongue, vocal cords"). *Glot* family members include *polyglot*, *glossary*, and of course *glossolalia*, "speaking in tongues."

Don't confuse Hamelin's medieval rodent management services with today's Pied Piper start-up in *Silicon Valley*, whose product uses an "algorithm that initially fielded Weisman Scores™ nearing the theoretical limit of lossless compression models for Lempel-Ziv-Welch in .gif files." Heady stuff.

Algorithm, incidentally, commemorates the Arabic mathematician *al-Khwarizmi*. Between the eighth and tenth centuries, while Europe wallowed in the post-Roman mud of the Dark Ages, Persia was where the math action was.

Not surprising. Computation in Roman numerals doesn't bear thinking about. *Arabic numerals* originated in Babylon twenty-two centuries ago, when Roman numerals were still the hot thing—which, given the Romans' melt-prone wax tablets, makes an unhappy metaphor. Returning to numbers, the Romans used a small tablet, *tabula* (Italian preferred *tavola*, table) for tabulation.

Returning to the Pied Piper: Two to three centuries after the Hameln tragedy, a German manuscript reported that 1) on June 26, 1284, 130 children were lured away by a sinister piper in clothes of many colors. 2) They were "lost" (*verloren*, like "forlorn") at a "calvary"—very sinister indeed. *Calvary*, from Latin *calvaria*, "cranium," is the hill where Christ was crucified, which the Gospel calls the "Place of the Skull" and which the tongue tangles with the more common *cavalry*. The story goes that two children who escaped ratted him out, appropriately, to the Hamelners.

To repeat my tiresome axiom, the Pied Piper legend surely has a kernel of truth. By the way, saying "kernel" for *colonel* seems weird, but *colonel*'s root is Latin *columnella*, a smallish column (literally "little big neck"), i.e., the troops led by one military officer. The French morphed him into a "coronel," and we spell it Latin and pronounce it French.

And here's a military mutation I don't get: *troops*. A troop is a group of soldiers. So how can thirty-eight *troops* die in a battle? So now a troop is *one* soldier? (And don't confuse *troop* with a *troupe* of performing artists.)

Incidentally, the term *G.I.* for a soldier (enlisted man, not an officer) started as "Government Issue" or "General Issue"—a soldier's equipment. A soldier was called a *G.I. Joe* well before Hasbro produced their boy-doll "action" figure in 1964.

But we keep wandering from the Pied Piper. Since the legend must have a historical basis, did the Hameln kids perish wholesale in a plague? Did they drown? Scholars have floated the notions of landslide or sinkhole. Others suggest they were kidnapped to join a religious sect or possibly a children's crusade. How about the usual suspects: a large-scale pederasty or child-slavery operation? There's a theory that they were among youths recruited to settle in areas (like today's Poland) annexed in the thirteenth century by the Germans (who have a long history of oozing eastward)—and this one's interesting: several academics back the colonization hypothesis by citing the number of Hameln surnames found today in these regions.

In memory of the children, it's illegal even today to play music or sing on Hameln's Bungelosenstrasse—"Drumless Street": *Der Sage nach führte der Rattenfänger die Kinder durch die Bunge-losenstraße aus der Stadt hinaus. Daraufhin wurde das Spielen von Musik in der Straße auf alle Zeit verboten.*

Naturally (or supernaturally) a couple of seventeenth-century writers ascribe the kids' exodus to the devil. À propos of evil German phenomena, *Geist* (cousin of "ghost") = spirit. You find it in *Zeitgeist*, "the spirit of the time." And in *Poltergeist*, "ghostly disturbance-maker." German nouns are capitalized, as were English nouns in the late seventeenth century and into the eighteenth; see the Declaration of Independence.

As for the children's *crusade* ("mission for the Cross"), consider Latin *crux* and *crucifix*. A *crux* is where its arms cross, the central point, whence it evolved into something *crucial*, central to success. Athletes are always tearing their ACLs and talking about it without knowing it's their X-shaped *anterior cruciate ligament*; crucifixion is a lot more *excruciating*.

Your *cruciferous* plants (broccoli, cabbage, cauliflower, Brussels sprouts) have cross-shaped petals. Not to mention geography, where *Santa Cruz* = "holy cross" and a *cruise* = "a crossing." The surnames of painter Dela*croix*, singer Jim *Croce*, and actors

Penelope *Cruz* and Tom *Cruise* honor the cross in French, Italian, Spanish, and English.

Let's return to the rat, always the villain of the plot, have you met Templeton in *Charlotte's Web*? The crook among crooks is the Mafioso who *rats out* other mobsters.

Except rodents aren't all bad.

The Greek Herodotus, "the Father of History," credits the expulsion of Sennacherib from Jerusalem to mice who gnawed to shreds the Assyrians' bowstrings and other military assets. Stranger things have happened, maybe. The book of Kings explains Sennacherib's defeat differently: "the angel of the Lord went out, and smote in the camp of the Assyrians an hundred fourscore and five thousand: and when they arose early in the morning, behold, they were all dead corpses"—as opposed to live corpses, unless they were following the script of *Night of the Living Dead*, a cult (literally) classic of 1968.

But Herodotus was also known as "the Father of Lies." Sennacherib had his moments. In Byron's version, "The Assyrian came down like the wolf on the fold / And his cohorts were gleaming in purple and gold." Anyway, he survived the mouse fiasco and turned Nineveh into a place of splendor (its remains largely trashed by ISIS in 2015).

27

Speaking of Which

Pronouns

Now let's talk about *you*, by which I mean the *pronoun*. If you squirm at the term as a bad school day memory, skim or skip the next few paragraphs.

Paragraph, by the way: Greek *para* = "beside," and *graph* = "write," as with a graphite pencil. *Photography* is "writing with light" (your *camera* is a *camera obscura*, "dark chamber"). *Graphology* is handwriting analysis, used by forensic investigators and formerly by some psychologists. I'm not sure about her professional credentials, but Aunty Flo says spiky tops on your *n* show intelligence and dishonesty. In a two-humped (non-dromedary) *n*, a larger first hump indicates quasi-narcissism. A left-slanting *n* shows "the writer's amazing dedication to some cause in their life, but anything there's always something and different about the subject." Something I *am* sure about is Aunty's writing skills. By the way, if you check her out online, don't confuse her with "Aunt Flo," a folksy euphemism for menstruation. Like soothsaying, this science is an opportunity for a moonlighting charlatan: gullibility exploitation is a market not yet saturated. *Graphic*, incidentally, means "clearly represented," not "violent."

Speak for Yourself. In today's English, *you* is the only *you*. Not so simple elsewhere. Latin had two *yous*: singular *tu* and plural *vos*. The non-Latinate Russian versions are ты and Вы respectively (the latter is pronounced *vih*). All four of these evolved from the same distant ancestor, namely PIE *yū*.

These languages also use the plural pronoun to address *one* person formally: the French use *vous*, reserving *tu* for a pal or family member. Spanish, too—familiar *tú* and formal *usted*.

In German and Italian it gets worse, with three *yous*: German has *du* (singular familiar), *ihr* (plural familiar), and *Sie* (third person used for *formal you* both singular and plural). This third-person form is a relic of times when we spoke to our betters like this: "Does your lordship prefer the yellow socks?" Some rulers are so great they can't fit into the first-person singular. Instead of *I*, a king would use the *royal we*, like President Trump when asked about his health: "No. We have no symptoms whatsoever."

Up to the seventeenth century, the English addressed a familiar person as *thou*. Elizabethans, for example, said *thou beest*, "you are" (like German *du bist*) and *thou dost* ("doeth"). *You* plural was once *ye*.

The *tu* forms can also reflect condescension. A lady addresses her servant with *tu*, for example, while the servant calls the lady *vous*. Or use it to insult someone of your own class. *You* protocol is a social minefield. At what point in a relationship does the informal form become appropriate?

You can get away with bloopers when burlesquing King James-style English. Your audience won't double over in derisive mirth if you use *thee* as sentence subject or *thou* as object. He *goeth* derives from the Latin third-person verb ending, thou *goest* from the second person. But nobody will leap like a startled hare when you say "I goeth" or "we goest."

For these old-fashioned irregular verbs the wise reader will make a laminated quick-reference card for wall or wallet.

It Says a Lot for Them. But English has a major drawback. Does one go around saying, "One should be careful when playing dodgeball"? One does not. One says "*you* should be careful." We need an impersonal French *on*.

28

Play on Words

Sports

Etymologically, "sport" originated in *disport* (amuse) from French *déporter*, to "take away," a synonym for *divert*, "turn away" (from workaday business).

Sports *fans* may not all be fanatics, but that's the source of *fan*; the meaning has weakened over time.

The archetypical athletic artifact is the *ball*. I mentioned above how "ball" and "phallus" are very close etymologically. Speaking of balls, it's Latin *pila*, "sphere," that generated the pharmacological *pill* (which today is often a *tablet*, flat rather than spherical), or a *capsule* (from Latin "small case"). We can also thank the *pila* for the inelegant *piles*, as in hemorrhoids (call St. Fiacre, see above). Other ball-like articles: *platoon* (a ball of people), *pellet*, and *peloton*, the main cluster of riders in a bike-race. Note: For $2,495 you can buy a high-end stationary bicycle, the *Peloton Bike+*, for "the holistic workout you crave." Or you can save the cash and spend an hour alongside Sisyphus in Hades.

If you've forgotten the *furlong*, it's equal to one Greek *stadion*—the length of a Roman *stadium*. The original sports *arena* was a Latin *harena*—sanded area. What Americans call a soccer *field* the British call a *pitch* (from the cricket term for the strip of lawn between wickets). British *football* is American *soccer*. The name arose from the game's early label *Association Football*, which was often abbreviated as *Assoc. Football* and then further shortened to "soc" (preferable to "ass," as one wag points out). Whatever. *Soccer* was an alternative to *rugger*—short for *rugby football.*

Tennis allegedly began as French *Tenez*, which means "Receive (this)." The sport evolved from an earlier indoor version, the *jeu de paume*, "game of the palm (of the hand)" *sans* a racket. But for your tennis *racket* you have Arabic to thank, where *rāḥat* = "palm of the hand." More French: a *raquette* is also a snowshoe.

In France, tennis has distinguished itself in culture and politics as well as the world of sport. In Paris, a former tennis court became the *Musée du Jeu de Paume*, a gallery of Impressionist painting which today houses contemporary art. (Speaking of Impressionists, several artists whose works were rejected in 1863 by the Paris *Salon* went on to create a *Salon des Refusés* to exhibit their pictures.) Commoners excluded from a political assembly met in 1789 at a royal tennis court near the Versailles palace, where they took *The Tennis Court Oath* for self-representation.

Squash took its name from its squishy ball, which is squishy only if compared to a solid rock.

Hockey used a "hook-like" stick.

Volleyball: The source of *volley* is French *volée*, "flight," as heard in the song "*Volare*," "to fly." Italian-Americans Dino Crocetti (1958) and Robert Ridarelli (1960) sang a cover version in English. The song was a mega-hit; and if these two artists aren't household names, it's because we know them as Dean Martin and Bobby Rydell respectively.

A three-paragraph parenthesis on stage and screen names: Remember Naples and Leghorn? Some entertainers who wanted to appeal to mid-century Middle America assumed an apple-pie kind of name. In the 1950s, there were many in the WASP-ish American audience who couldn't relate (or worse) to Italian names. Take just the name Francis: Dion was Dion Francis DiMucci. Connie Francis had been baptized as (the prettier)

Concetta Rosa Maria Franconero. Tony Bennett was born An-
thony Benedetto. Anne Bancroft, star of *The Graduate* (1967),
began life as Anna Italiano.

Luckily, American culture evolved, and xenophobia was not
why Stefani Germanotta went with Lady Gaga. Another who
just wanted marquee appeal was Norma Jeane Mortenson (Mar-
ilyn Monroe). Same with Alexandra Zuck (Sandra Dee), Doris
Mary Ann Kappelhoff (Doris Day), and Archibald Alec Leach
(Cary Grant).

Pre-Kardashians, Armenian was out; Arlene Francis was
short for Arline Francis Kazanjian. A star with a Jewish name?
Also too alien, especially when anti-Semitism prevailed in large
swaths of the country. Winona Ryder started out as Winona
Laura Horowitz, Bob Dylan as Robert Zimmerman. Ever heard
of Bernard Schwartz (Tony Curtis) or Belle Miriam Silverman
(Beverly Sills) or Benjamin Kubelsky (Jack Benny)?

But volleyball distracted me from sports:

Athletics today are all about *technology.* From Greek *techne,*
"art, technical skill"; the goddess *Techne* was patron of crafts.
To highlight Techne's immortality: Today you can meet her at
Camp Half-Blood Fanon (an online "roleplay group"), where we
learn "she did not have a particuarly [sic] interesting life . . .
Techne can most often be seen wearing a pair of paint-splat-
tered, accidentally-ripped jeans, a brightly colored tank top and
a cream cardigan, though when she is working she swaps the
last two for an old t-shirt and a painter's smock."

But back to our topic—sports. We're used to the technical
hoopla aimed at professional-sports audiences—expensive TV
visuals, ads, and company-endorsed gear. But consider a simple, ancient sport like fencing, which mass audiences don't find
electrifying—except it is: Electronically-sensitive sabers, foils,
and *lamés* (conductive jackets) monitor strikes and scores.

What with sports technology, the old-fashioned *umpire*
("non-peer" of the athletes) may become superfluous. As for the
coach, he or she can almost spend the game at a laptop. One

option for communication is the *Porta-Phone TD900HD 7-Coach System—Dual Channel* ($4,200), which targets high schools and college football teams. But this system is designed for amateur teams (strictly speaking, *amateur* = "lover" of something, thus not motivated by pay); pro-team systems are presumably pricier. Team members can even be wired up to provide their vital stats so that the coach can swap out a flagging player.

A marathoner must find Aristotle's "golden mean" between dehydration and *hyponatremai*, too little salt in the blood from over-hydration. In the periodic table, sodium is "Na" (from Latin *natrium*); hence salt = NaCl. And *salt* merits another small detour.

In the book of Matthew, Jesus warns the Disciples: "Ye are the salt of the earth: but if the salt have lost his savour, wherewith shall it be salted?" Call someone *salt of the earth* to describe a solid, reliable guy.

On the contrary, *salting the earth* is a scorched-earth tactic: Conquer a country and sow its fields with salt to spoil the soil long-term. The Roman policy *Carthago delenda est* dictated total and permanent crippling (as in deletion) of Carthage.

Salary goes back to the Romans, where a soldier's *salarium* was money for buying *sal* (salt) and where an underperformer wasn't *worth his salt*. And he needed salt—to keep food from going bad and to make (bad) food palatable. *Salad* originated with *herba salata*, a salty vegetable-dish.

In a 77 A.D. book, Pliny the Elder suggests that the great King Mithridates, for one, used to take his supper *with a grain of salt (addito salis grano)* as a poisoning preventative; good luck with that. (This may have been paranoia; but then power is often inversely proportional to popularity.) When you're seated at dinner *below the salt*, you haven't made it onto the A-list near the head of the table. An unkind character might not only injure you but *rub salt into the wound*.

Put salt on someone's tail to prevent him from getting away. An old notion said salting a bird's tail kept it from flying. PETA

(People for the Ethical Treatment of Animals) would not go for this. PETA is what we like to see in an acronym: The letters form a word that reflects what the acronym stands for, in this case "pet." (MADD—Mothers Against Drunk Driving—is another.) Or consider the "Amber Alert" system, credited with a 64% success rate, which took its title from the tragedy of a murdered child named Amber. After its launch, they gave it a *backronym* (the acronym-ization of an existing term) whereby AMBER stands for *America's Missing: Broadcast Emergency Response.*

Nowadays, by the way, proper hydration goes well beyond salt. The Gatorade Sports Science Institute and the oxymoronic agency The Coca Cola Beverage Institute of Health and Wellness have, philanthropically, sponsored conferences for the learned American College of Sports Medicine, which in a game-changing study recommends drinks with electrolytes and carbohydrates.

Running is not a breathtaking spectator sport; even celebrated *marathons* are mostly inaccessible to viewers. In 490 B.C.E., the Greeks defeated the Persians at Marathon (which means "field of fennel"). To announce the victory, a messenger sprinted the 26.2 miles to Athens without resting. He also dropped dead upon arrival, which supports my opinion that marathoners are awe-inspiring and insane.

Another non-team sport is shooting. You can fire at living things or practice on moving targets called "clay pigeons," also called *skeet*: both *shoot* and *skeet* are cousins of Dutch "schieten" and "skieten." Other derivations include the *shuttle*, the thing that "shoots" back and forth across a loom (hence a vehicle that travels to and fro). What gets more airtime is the versatile "*shoot!*" as a euphemism for "*shit!*"

A *shuttlecock*, aka *birdie*, is what you shoot over the badminton net. The Duke of Beaufort lived at *Badminton House* where badminton was first played. But take care not to confuse this Beaufort with the Irishman Francis Beaufort, who invented the *Beaufort Wind Scale*, which measures wind force from "Light

Air," to "Fresh Breeze," to "Near Gale," to "Violent Storm," to "Hurricane"—more vivid than miles per hour.

Croquet was named for the mallet's resemblance to a shepherd's crook. The *mallet* itself is a "hammer" (Latin *malleus*). *Malleable* seems almost the opposite, but a malleable item is "beat-able," as by a blacksmith. The Irish pronounce croquet *crookey*; the English pronounce it *crokey*; Americans say *croKAY*.

29

The Name of the Game

Talking Points

But is croquet a *sport* or just a tame *game?*

At last, a chapter only a few inches long.

Wordplay. I'm well qualified to discuss games for the sedentary. Middle English *gamen*, "game," gave us *gamble*, which you do at a *casino*, a "little house." Its homonym *gambol*, however, we inherit from *gamba*, the "leg" discussed above almost *ad nauseam.*

In playing cards the *clubs* suit derives, unsurprisingly, from "clover." We've looked at the etymologies of spades and diamonds. As for *hearts*, whether card or bodily organ, I'm willing to trek back to the PIE for "heart," *kerd*, which sprouted into not only German *herz* but also Latin *cor, cordis*; French *coeur*; even Russian *сердце* (transliterated "serdtse"); and probably Gaelic *cridhe*. (Heinrich *Hertz* gave us a homonym for *herz*; a *hertz* is a frequency of one cycle/second, and we'll stop right there with the physics and acknowledge John D. Hertz, founder of the Hertz Drive-Ur-Self System, and that is not a typo in there.)

As for board games, *backgammon* ≈ "backwards-game," which may mean something to you if you play. The early Romans called their backgammon-like game *alea*—"game of chance." More generically, *alea* meant "die," as in "dice." In a single event (49 B.C.E.) Julius Caesar gave us two modern metaphors:

1) *the die is cast* (*alea iacta est*), which he said when he
2) *crossed the Rubicon*

In crossing this "red-hued," river, he entered Italy. But the Romans didn't allow generals returning from foreign wars to bring their armies into the country; a leader with troops at his disposal was a dicey thing. The ambitious Caesar, hot to tackle the kingpin Pompey, dithered but proceeded. Caesar's move *burned his bridges* politically.

My son always assumed "the die is cast" referred to the process of *die casting*—a process not invented till nineteen centuries later, where a *die* (origin unknown) is a mold. Since a mold determines the future product, his interpretation makes sense (see above, "taking for granite").

For some reason Jeep Wrangler named a recent model *Rubicon Hard Rock Edition*. This car's Premium Alpine Nine-Speaker System would have interested Caesar: The Alps (as well as the *Rubicon* river) marked the Gaul-Italy boundary. The Jeep Rubicon is the "Flagship of the Wrangler fleet," surely overkill for the namesake of a small Italian stream. And Caesar would have no truck with the Jeep Gladiator, which is neither captive nor slave. Plus, what good is "Weekend Warrior Mode" to him when his calendar lacks weekends?

Speaking of fleets, Nissan's *Armada* is not only automotive but amphibious! And plural!—not one battleship but an armed *fleet*. This would make it a "bundled" product (from *byndelle*, Old English "binding"); I guess you can't buy just one unit.

But I was supposed to be writing a few paragraphs on games.

Greek "dice" = *kybos*, "cube." The name of the game *dominoes* goes back to medieval Italy, where the Lone-Ranger style domino mask became standard Carnival wear that resembled the headgarb of French clergy called *domini*. By the way, *carnival* = *carne* + *vale*: "farewell to meat" for Lent.

Parenthesis on dominoes: In the late 1890s, the American Sugar Refining Company changed its name to the Domino Sugar Corporation; one of their leading products was solid rectangles of sugar the size and shape of a domino, bisected by a groove for easy dividing. The company later lost a trademark-infringement suit against Domino's Pizza (originally named DomiNick's after Dominick DiVarti).

.

30

In Glowing Terms

Colors

Poets are partial to "pied": Gerard Manley Hopkins wrote about "Pied Beauty." Shakespeare sings of summer's "daisies pied and violets blue" in the same poem where "greasy Joan doth keel the pot," which my father quoted kitchenside while I washed the dishes. We've met the P. Piper.

Pre-chemical dyes contributed plenty of color-words. The source of *crimson* is the pulverized body of the very unattractive female *kermes* insect. Another prime producer of red dye was the medieval Tuscan town San Gimignano, famous for its defensive towers. (*Tuscan* evolved from *Etruscan*; Italian *Toscano* also gave the operatic *Tosca* her name; the popularity of Tuscany's Chianti region with the English led to the nickname *Chiantishire*.) In San Gimignano the saffron plant was used to dye long bolts of cloth (red, not yellow). The city towers, built ever-higher in military one-upsmanship with other towns, came in handy for suspending the fabric to dry.

Enough said about red, except to mention the fanciful *Dr. Red*, as in "Paging Dr. Red. Dr. Red, please report to Elevator B"—hospital code-speak for "fire in Elevator B." Regarding fire: a *pyramid* is "flame-shaped," derived from Greek *pyr* as in "pyre."

Yellow, German *gelb*, Italian *giallo*, and Spanish *amarillo* are etymologic cousins to our friend *gall*, if you care to remember the aforementioned yellow bile (an inflamed gallbladder turns your skin yellow). All these yellows descend from *ghel*, another PIE term that's straightforward enough to approach with aplomb.

If I were really malevolent, I'd drop two words here: "Mellow Yellow," a song which when heard makes itself at home in your brain for possibly weeks, if not life. The chart-topping artist Donovan should go boil his head.

All I'm saying about *green* is 1) PIE *ghre* ("to become green") evolved into both "green" and "grow." 2) Your *salad days* are your youth, when you're "green." Cleopatra regrets an affair she had with Caesar back in her "salad days, when I was green in judgement." 3) Speaking of plays, the *green room* where actors wait offstage may, and it's a stretch, have originally contained plants beneficial to elocution. An aside, *ovation* probably descends from the Greek word *euaizin* ("shout with pleasure," as the *eu-* suggests). Nowadays the *standing O* suffers from ovation inflation.

Blue notes: *turquoise* means "from Turkey." *Once in a blue moon* alludes to the infrequency of two full moons in one calendar month. *Cyanide* (in a chemical reaction) appears dark blue (Greek *kyanos*), just as *cyanosis*, lack of blood oxygen, turns the skin blue. Forced to choose, I'd go yellow with gall or red with shame.

On *violet*: If you're *born to the purple*, you're rich enough to wear purple robes dyed by secretions of the murex snail. Tyrian reddish-purple was imported from the city Tyre in *Phoenicia*. Consider *amethyst*: its Greek prefix "*a*" denotes "not." The *a-methyst* stone (*a* + *meth*) was supposed to keep you from getting high—Greek *meth*, as in methamphetamines, means "drunken." We owe *maroon*, brownish-red, to chestnuts, as in *marrons glacés*—candied chestnuts. *Lavender* we've discussed.

We can track *white* back to PIE *kweit* or *kweid-o*. Along the way we run into German *weiss*, from the older *hwiz*. And all the way down to Old English, this root carries the sense of "shining." The French borrowed *blanc*, "white," from Frankish-Germanic *blank*. *Carte blanche*, like "blank check," gives you a metaphor for doing whatever you want.

A *candidate* was originally a *candidatus*, who wore a white—*candidus*—toga while campaigning to become a Roman *senator*. (For this office you were required to be *senex*, "senior.") As for *candle*, it's a thing that burns bright white—incandescently. Speaking of which, old-time workaholics *burned the candle at both ends* by balancing it on a horizontal stick; sometimes you need more light than one shrimp candle-flame. When you pull an all-nighter, you exhaust yourself. Burning the candle at both ends, however, originally meant to exhaust a precious resource, namely candle wax. Excessive nocturnal light was a wasteful luxury. Eye strain? Deal with it.

Incidentally, remember the *g* sound becoming *j*: With words inherited from Latin, our pronunciation of certain consonants depends on their route to English. We get Latin's hard *c* in *candle, cat, canine, cap*, and *escape*. Other words pass through Norman tongues which move the *c* (like the *g* > *j*) up-mouth into the mushier *ch* of *chandelier, chat, chien, chapeau, échapper*. Chicken Cacciatore is hunter-style chicken (Italian *caccia* = a hunt). Traveling north to France, the *c* softened to *chasse*, thence to our "chase." On the other hand, we acquired "catch" and "capture" directly from Latin *captiare* before it ever got to France. Latin *captiare* sounds like "cap-tee-aray." But I've mentioned that child spelling *tree* as *chree*: the tongue doesn't take the trouble to move toothwards, and the staccato T slurs into *ch*, a sound that Italian *cacciare* took on.

While we're on night-time candles: you may already know that *curfew* dates from medieval *couvre-feu*, the time for covering your fire to prevent a house fire while you slept. What about *night*? Its *-ght* shows English's German heritage. *Nacht* = night. *Macht*, as in *Wehrmacht* (literally war-power) = mightiness. *Recht* = right. *Licht*, light.

Another German digraph, gnarly for young spellers, is *kn*, as in *know*. That *kn* is a relative of the Greek stem *gno-* that gives us *agnostic, ignore,* and *diagnosis.*

I'll conclude the color catalogue with *black*. This word is another example of the *b* > *f* consonant shift; it's a cognate of Latin *flagrare*, as in *conflagration*, in the sense of blackened by fire. Both go back to Greek *phleg* (above we mentioned the burning Phlegethon River in Hades). *Flagrare* also gives us *flagrant*, "burning," related to *in flagrante delicto* (in the very act of a crime).

That's *black*. English also uses other, Germanic, words denoting blackness. *Schwarz* = "black" in German and gives us our *swarthy*. *Sordid* is an etymological cousin.

31

Say When

Telling Time

To begin with a homonym for a calendar *date*, let's consider the fruit date, which supposedly looks like a finger (*dactyl* in Greek), and it would be an unpleasantly pudgy one. The date may take its name from an Arabic cognate to *dactyl—daqal* (I always feel a twinge of envy of the Arabs, who dispense with our tedious post-*q u*). As for the *date palm* tree, its splayed fronds are said to resemble the palm of a hand.

But our topic here is time. The calendar *date* is a "given"— like *data*, from Latin "to give." "A.D." is the abbreviation of the Latin *anno domini*: "in the year of our Lord." The Christian-centric A.D. is being replaced by C.E., "Common Era," meaning the last 2000 years. Same with B.C., "Before Christ"—now commonly B.C.E. (Before the Common Era). *Annus* (year) branched across Europe into *anno*, *año*, and *année*, evolving divergently, much as animal forelimbs evolved into arms, fins, and wings.

A parenthesis on *wings*: Planes have "little wings" that are called *ailerons*, from *aile*, French "wing." So don't say *airelons*, temptingly airborne though it sounds. On the other hand, *Airylon* would be a good name for a breathable synthetic fabric.

Doubtless you know that *a.m.* = *ante meridiem* ("before midday") and *p.m.* = *post meridiem*. You may also be up on month-names, so feel free to sit out the next set.

In the Long Term. Months were formerly *moonths*, since one *moon* cycle takes one month. (German *Mond*, by the way, is *moon*'s cognate.)

Our months are Roman:

January: Janus, the god with two faces, who oversaw beginnings and endings (like the new and just-ended year) and who gave us our *janitors—custodians*, "guards of entrances and gates."

February: Februus, god of purification by burning, related to Latin *febris*, "fever."

March: Mars, god of war and martial affairs.

April: Latin *aperire*, "to open" (recall *apéritif*) as in blossoms.

May: Maia, a Roman fertility goddess.

June: Juno.

July: Julius Caesar.

August: Roman emperor Augustus's lucky period.

September–December: Latin numbers 7–10. The Roman calendar had 10 months.

Call It a Day. Four days of our week honor Norse gods:

Tuesday: war-god Tyr; interesting, since Italian *martedi* and French *mardi* are also named for the Roman war god.

Wednesday: *Odin*, alias *Woden*, who gives the day its funky spelling.

Thursday: *Thor*. Like Jove (Italian *giovedi*, French *jeudi*), Thor manages lightning and thunderbolts.

Friday: *Freyja*, goddess of Love. Romance-language Fridays go with their own Venus.

Non-Norse days:

Monday, moon-day, like French *lundi*.

Saturday, Saturn's day.

Sunday. Never mind—needs PIE.

A *holiday* was a "holy day." Holidays mean Hallmark: In eighteenth-century London, the seal of the Goldsmiths' *Hall* assured the quality of gold with their *hallmark*.

Valentine's Day: First of all, the Valentine we honor may have been at least two different men. One St. Valentine was a decapitated cleric. According to another tale, the priest Valentine illegally married girls and soldiers, although the Roman emperor had decreed the army a bachelor institution. A third Valentine story describes the goings-on in the Roman festival of Lupercalia in mid-February, when bachelors drew the names of single girls out of a pot. Yet another alleges a later origin: Chaucer says that birds mate on February 14. So take your pick.

Lent: The days begin to *lengthen*.

Easter derives from PIE *aus*, meaning "to shine," as in sunrise; Easter (cousin of German *Ostern*) started as a feast-day honoring the vernal equinox.

Halloween: November 1 is All Saints' Day. The night before is *All Hallows' Eve*, "hallowed e'en."

Chanukah/Hanukkah (Hebrew for "consecration") honors the rededication of the Second Temple. The Hebrew *Menorah* and Arabic *minaret* both descend from Semitic *manarah*, "light(house)."

Christmas: Christ's Mass. The ocean current *El Niño* that influences the weather around Christmas-time, by the way, means "The [Christ] Child."

Don't Tell a Soul. On *Groundhog Day* the woodchuck's shadow goes clairvoyant. February 2nd got a PR boost from Ghostbuster Bill Murray, specialist in *ectoplasm* ("external fluid")—the aura issuing from a supernatural body.

32

Body Language

From Hand to Mouth

Starting at ground level, the *foot* (the rough size of a man's foot) settled during the Middle Ages at about 13.2 inches.

Ankle = angle. The ankle bone is Latin *talus*; it's where a predatory bird grows its *talons*. A good brand name for running shoes would be *talaria*—Mercury's winged sandals. Myths prevail: the Achilles' tendon connects the muscles of your heel and calf. Metaphorically, an *Achilles' heel* is a weakness. Achilles' mother, the sea-nymph Thetis, had a way with water. To make her infant son invulnerable, she dipped him head-first into the River Styx, and it worked, except for his heel where she'd held onto him.

Achilles ended up at Troy, despite his mother's draft-dodging ploy—dressing him as a girl. Odysseus showed up on a recruiting mission and blew the fake girl's cover when he caught her admiring not the tchotchkes he'd brought as gifts but the weapons. During the ensuing war, helicopter mom Thetis swooped down to the battlefield and gave Achilles armor forged by the Olympian blacksmith Hephaestus; fatally, however, the armor left his vulnerable heel exposed. By the way, *helicopter* = *helico* ("spiraling") + *ptero* ("wing," like "pterodactyl"); one of their nicknames is "whirlybird."

The seat of your soul was once in the *sacrum* in your lower back—the "holy bone." Its Greek name was *hieron osteon*. (Greek *hiera,* "sacred," spawned *hierarchy,* a theological ranking system that describes the echelons not only of clergy but also of angels—your *seraphim, cherubim,* and *archangels,* to name a few.)

By the way, if your name is *Jerome,* you're really *Hieronymus,* "holy name" in Greek. In Spanish you're *Gerónimo*—also the Mexican epithet for an Apache chief named Goyathlay. This individual, while performing a stuntmanly leap, allegedly yelled *Gerónimo!*—a cry echoed by World War II parachutists as they jumped.

Getting back to backs, you get your *vertebrae* from Latin *vertere,* "turn"—same as the *versus* of the direction-changing oxen. The vertebrae act as your torso's hinge.

Your hand has a lot to do with being human. A lucky fluke in the genes ended up as the opposable thumb, allowing primates to evolve into *homo erectus.* They're not just practical, either: think only of the flamenco guitar handiwork of *Manitas de Plata*—"little silver hands."

For *head,* remember the verbal descendants of the prolific Latin *caput, capitis.* In PIE, where in this case I can venture without trepidation, "head" was *kaput.* A thing that's *kaput* is as dead as someone *decapitated.* A Germanic cognate is *haupt,* as in German *Hauptmann,* "head officer"—or "captain," which also derives from *caput.*

33

Strange to Say

Mixed Messages. Spell-checkers are *sophomoric* ("knowledge-morons") crutches that inspire false confidence. English, where Latinate and Anglo-Saxon converge, is an exceptionally rich language, which leaves a lot of room for *orthographic* (from Greek *ortho,* "correct") errors.

Homonyms have the same sound. High-ranking homonym hazards: *lead/led, pour/pore, discrete/discreet, complimentary/complementary, peak/peek/pique.* Two homonym hitches I read just this week: 1) "White House officials *poured over* data on testing." 2) Something *peaked the curiosity* of an author unaware of the word *pique,* "to prick." Some—many—writers mistakenly use the contraction *it's* where they mean *its* (*it's*'s apostrophe suggesting the possessive *'s*). On the other hand, it's often through carelessness, as is confusing *your* and *you're* and *too* for *two.*

Homographs—"same *spelling*"—can also spell trouble: "The lacerates were running down his face." Aside from being a nice line of blank verse, that sentence comes from a high-school essay by George W. Bush who, seeking a synonym for *tears* (of sadness), plucked from his thesaurus the verb *to tear,* meaning "to rip up."

Then we have a pair of diametrically opposed hacking verbs. *Hew,* "split apart with an axe," also means "adhere to" ("stick to, comply with"). The second hatchet pair: *Cleave* means both "split" and "adhere."

Speaking of splitting, *sanction* also undergoes a *schism*. Both senses of the word go back to Latin *sanctus*, "made holy." *To sanction* is "to declare acceptable." But you can do a 180 by declaring *sanctions* against something you *don't* sanction.

In the apparent-oxymoron department, we have *spendthrift*. At first blush the word seems riven by internal strife. But no; *thrift* derives from the verb *thrive*—to prosper: a spendthrift fritters away his prosperity. A *skinflint*, however, is so miserly he tries to skin flakes off a hard flint.

To Say the Least. With quantity, let's begin with *unique*. It stems from *unus*. There's only ONE of something that's "unique." You can't say "very unique." It is or it isn't the only one. Speaking of which, today's paper called something "very binary." No! A *binary* thing exists on or off, with exactly two possibilities. *Binoculars* have two eyepieces, unless Argus Panoptikos, the Greek hundred-eyed giant, ordered a custom pair (except his optician couldn't call them "a pair"). A bisexual sticks with male and female partners. Your *biceps* has two "heads." *-Ceps* is another form of the Latin word *caput*. And consider Latin *cephalicus*, from Greek "related to the head."

Bigamy isn't quite polygamy. Your *bicuspids* have two points.

Plurals, perils. Say you say "one *criteria* for judging." You can't, because "criteria" is plural. You can use one *criterion* to judge something. Same with *phenomenon/phenomena*. To the individual who mentioned that "mental illness still has a *stigmata*": a *stigma*, yes—but the plural *stigmata* usually refers to "the wounds of the crucified Christ." *Data* is plural (its singular is one *datum*, a fact (from Latin "given thing"). Lately even the layperson hears the technical lingo giving *data* its plural verb, and it sounds very scientific and impressive. How to use it yourself: "These data support the jellyfish-mite as a vector of the common cold." *Jellyfish*—a lovely word and even better than its scientific name *Medusa*.

Who Says? Shibboleths: A *shibboleth* (Hebrew) is a plant part. But Hebrews used the word as a test for identifying an enemy. Scene: the Book of Judges. The Gileadites encounter an Ephraimite:

> Then said they unto him, Say now Shibboleth: and he said Sibboleth: for he could not frame to pronounce *it* right. Then they took him, and slew him at the passages of Jordan: and there fell at that time of the Ephraimites forty and two thousand.

A slick maneuver. WWII G.I.s used to make a possible Japanese spy pronounce lollapalooza.

Crosswords. An Oxford vicar gave his name to *spoonerisms*: May I sew you to another sheet? Does your bike have a well-boiled icicle chain? Our old friend Margaret, the "pearl," might cast swirls before pine. I like to refer to one of my books, *The Size of Happiness*, as *The Highs of Sappiness*.

Getting a Word in Edgewise: Portmanteaux. A *portmanteau* is literally a French "coat-carrier," namely a "trunk." Your trunk, for example, might contain the portmanteau-term *athleisure* wear—clothes made from athletic-wear fabrics but designed also for all-day wear. Lewis Carroll coined the term *portmanteau*: a word with "two meanings packed up in one word." I've mentioned *jeggings* for "jean-leggings," *furlong* for "furrow-long," *bit* for "binary digit." Other familiar ones: You can merge *tar* with its engineer John *McAdam* into *tarmacadam*, or *tarmac*. Governor Elbridge Gerry *gerrymandered* a voting district into a *salamander* shape.

To venerable terms like *motel* (motor-hotel), *brunch* (breakfast-lunch) and *smog* (smoke-fog), we've added *frenemy* (friend-enemy), a useful expression long overdue.

Then there are the commercial products. *Saran* Wrap honors the inventor's wife and daughter—Sarah and Ann. The air-freshener *Febreze* (hydroxypropyl beta-cyclodextrine) is a lame attempt at evoking fabric + breeze, and the only thing worse than its name is its odor. The *Chunnel* (the Channel Tunnel) nicely evokes a chugging train.

But a prize to the final piece of squalor: the revolting *cremains* (cremated remains). A suitable place to end.

34

Even as We Speak

Now You're Talking

The words that brought us to where we are today are forever sprouting new roots, where *sprout* is a cognate of both "sperm" and "spread."

Some English terms have spread around the globe. Take *OK*. The origin of *OK/Okay* is disputed, but most believe it started with Martin Van Buren, nicknamed "Old Kinderhook" from his home town *Kinderhook* (Dutch for "children's corner"). Others say OK originated in a nineteenth-century misspelling joke, "orl korrect." Hilarious, huh?

A word is no more than an insubstantial vowel-consonant sound. It's hardly even a breath-worth of air. But vocabulary is history. Imagine that the only access we had to the past was tracing the mutations in our language through the ages. I say we'd do okay: More than wars and political borders, more than carbon-dated bones and artifacts, words tell how our ancestors led their ordinary or extra-ordinary lives.

A word is not a snapshot but a millennia-long video.

Words are on the move even as we speak.

What route will they take? Forget GPS; Siri can't give you directions where there's no direction.

And you can't stop language, because *when all's said and done* is never.

CPSIA information can be obtained
at www.ICGtesting.com
Printed in the USA
JSHW030432131222
34796JS00001B/2

9 781589 881570